To Velma Milledge-Sanders

It's Time To Posses
The Land!!!

Jerrauld M Sanders
9-12-09

The Physics *of* **Money**

IF
YOU'VE
GOT
MY DOLLAR,

by Jerroll M. Sanders

I DON'T

ECONOMIC PROSPERITY &

IMPROVED RACE RELATIONS

Publisher's Cataloging-in-Publication Data
(*Provided by Quality Books, Inc.*)
Sanders, Jerroll M.
    The physics of money : if you've got my dollar, I
  don't : economic prosperity & improved race relations /
  by Jerroll M. Sanders. — 1st ed.
    p. cm.
    ISBN: 0-9708211-0-7

    1. African Americans—Economic conditions.   2. United
  States—Race relations—Economic aspects.   I. Title.

  E185.8.S26 2001   330.973'008996073
                               QBI01-200102

Printed in the United States of America

IF YOU'VE GOT MY DOLLAR, I DON'T

TABLE OF CONTENTS

TABLE OF CONTENTS

Acknowledgments

Ever since I was first called a nigger at age 5, I have had a book in my heart. As I stood looking at the little White girl who mouthed the racial epithet, I frowned, knowing that her actions required correction. But who would fulfill the task?

Years later, racial epithets are still around, sometimes spoken, more often thought. And just as racial epithets linger on, so do my memories of encounters with people who remind me of that little girl I met so long ago: The police who emptied money from my father's pockets along a dark Tennessee road hundreds of miles from home. The teacher who despised my good academic performance. And the manager who slowed my progress while undeserving Whites moved ahead.

My discoveries about being Black in America are ever unfolding. I have gone from the glass ceiling that prevented my upward climb in corporate America to a glass door that complicates my entrance into the business arena. I persist nevertheless, believing, like so many African-American business owners, that one day the door might open—at least enough for me to wiggle through.

I have continued my struggle with racism, trying to find my balance. First, I took on the robe of a racist, but the garment did not fit. So I redirected my anger toward God. After all, how does a God who claims to be Lord of all disenfranchise my entire race? And then, I got it! Racism—though practiced by mankind—is not ordained by God. So man, not God, is accountable.

ACKNOWLEDGMENTS

With racism reconciled but unresolved, I continue my journey as a Black woman in America. I am constrained by the knowledge that there are good White folks, yet compelled by the degree to which my Blackness affects my everyday life. But it was a horrific business event that drove me to rise late at night and early in the morning to put these thoughts to paper.

This is not a feel-good book because I call it as I see it. It is much like a bitter pill—hard to swallow but designed to cure. If you are not African-American, I hope you will endure the feelings this book might evoke and allow your views and attitudes to be changed fundamentally. If you are African-American, I hope you can begin your healing by taking control of your life.

Speaking of life, I pay tribute to people I shall never forget: Ms. Whitman, now deceased, who paid for my piano lessons when my parents fell upon hard times; my elementary school principal, Mr. Thomas, who applauded my every accomplishment; Tom P., a customer to whom color seemed like a button on a jacket—simply an accent; Renée H., for her tireless support, incredible devotion, and enormous skill; Roger Brown, a smart mind and an incredible friend; Nailah Hardrick, an example of what you can be when you have neither boots nor straps; and to my parents and family, who helped me know and appreciate what I am and who I am.

Finally, I thank the people of all colors I have met along the way who preserve my belief in the goodness and kindness of the human spirit.

Jerroll M. Sanders

Improved Race Relations

Improved race relations in America are not possible until African Americans gain economic strength. **African Americans will abandon their distrust of Whites** *when they know their success hinges not on the good deeds of Whites, but on a system of fair play that allows African Americans to run the same race as others—governed by the same rules, eligible for the same rewards.*

PREPARE YOUR MIND

"Race matters when the subject is wealth."
Dr. Cornel West

Taking on the Challenge

Racism is here to stay. It is a condition of the heart, a flaw in perception and moral character. Government cannot legislate it away and man cannot protest it away.

TAKING ON THE CHALLENGE

This book helps African Americans improve their economic condition. The African-American civil rights anthem "We Shall Overcome," like most long-standing themes, has become old and tired. Despite years of protesting, marching, and insisting on racial equality, the reality is that things have not changed— at least not very much for African Americans. So why do we continue getting the same poor results? We are working the wrong plan!

African Americans must replace their longtime focus on racial equality with a determination to gain financial strength, individually and as a community. We must carry out—all on our own, step-by-step—a process that enables more African Americans to become major deal-doers and owners of multiplexes, shopping malls, banks, office buildings, corporations, and other significant wealth-bearing holdings.

IF YOU'VE GOT MY DOLLAR, I DON'T

THE VALUE OF THIS APPROACH

Why, you may ask, should the approach in this book yield different results? It focuses on something African Americans can change: our economic condition. For decades, African Americans have mistakenly believed there is *something we can do, something we can be,* or *something we can become* that will convince America that we deserve a slice of the economic pie. African Americans have failed to realize they are engaged in a fierce competition that is designed to keep African Americans and other disadvantaged Americans where they are—and members of the White establishment, where they are.

Daily in America, there is an all-out competition among Asians, Whites, African Americans, Hispanics, and others for wealth. The more dollars you have, the more wealthy you are—and the more privileges you enjoy! Those who have wealth are in control. They have designed the system to perpetuate their wealth and control. Since there are only so many dollars available at a given time, increasing the wealth of African Americans ultimately means decreasing the wealth of those who are advancing economically at African Americans' expense. Diverting wealth to the African-American community requires a no-holds-barred approach to acquiring wealth.

COMPETING IN A LAND OF OPPORTUNITY

America is a land of opportunity. Ethnic groups come to America from the world over and attain significant wealth because they are not sidetracked by peripheral issues, such as racism and equality. They understand their goal and their purpose: to attain wealth. Interestingly, many members of these groups achieve staggering wealth in short periods of time.

Like it or not, you are in a fierce competition for economic wealth. If you compete effectively, you can take first prize. If you do not, you will surely lag behind.

The Nature of Competition

PREPARE YOUR MIND

"Strategy without tactics is the slowest route to victory. Tactics without strategy is the noise before defeat."

Sun Tzu

THE NATURE OF COMPETITION

Ethical Competitors

In the course of fierce competition, you will encounter ethical competitors *who will play by the rules of the game* and hostile competitors *who will not.*

Ethical competitors have a strong sense of fairness and moral fiber. You can classify them as Pillars of Democracy or Game Plan Observers.

- *Pillars of Democracy.* Even when isolated and rejected by their own for doing what is fair and appropriate, these pillars of democracy stand up for what their enlightened eyes see as wrong. They make a difference by insisting on fair play—people like the late Senator Robert F. Kennedy; the late federal court judge Frank Johnson, Jr., whose rulings in the 1950s and '60s helped end segregated buses, schools, parks, and restaurants in the South; the late Ralph McGill, editor and publisher of the *Atlanta Constitution,* who championed civil rights in the South during an era when, according to one source, it was "considered traitorous if not downright unhealthy"; and the many ethical competitors you encounter daily who, by their actions, create a playing field where ability, not race, determines outcome.

- *Game Plan Observers.* These competitors play by the rules of the game and let performance and process dictate outcome. They are a source of good, healthy competition.

IF YOU'VE GOT MY DOLLAR, I DON'T

THE NATURE OF COMPETITION

Hostile Competitors

Hostile competitors regard economic competition as an individual sport. The first and foremost rule is to compete to win; the second is to help team members. This strategy means seek your own economic advancement and then give preference to others in your race. This game plan has been carried out, day in and day out, throughout America for decades, and it has oppressed an entire race of African descendants living in America. While some hostile competitors actively work to deny African Americans opportunities, others simply ignore African Americans' appeals for fairness. These competitors are so encased in their perceptions and economic class that they simply do not want to hear about the perils of being Black in America. In fact, the mere mention of racism or discrimination makes them cringe, and they do not hesitate to let you know it.

In response, African Americans retreat, fearing they will be considered troublemakers, difficult, or unworthy of the economic advantages competitors can toss their way. So African Americans tolerate the gross unfairness, growing more disgusted by the day. And hostile competitors, fearing no repercussions, engage in more and more blatant infractions.

THE NATURE OF COMPETITION

Hostile Competitors

Hostile competitors include:

- *Subtle Interferers.* These competitors, in the deepest chambers of their hearts, believe that African Americans have a "place." They simply cannot fathom an African American being in a better economic position than they. Their perspective subtly guides their actions, preventing them from directing any substantial opportunities your way.

- *Ethics Violators.* These competitors commit minor process infractions that are just significant enough to give members of their race an unfair competitive advantage. These competitors appear to be operating fairly when in fact they are not.

- *Race Observers.* The goal of these competitors is to advance their own race while stifling African Americans. They flagrantly violate established rules, processes, and laws to dictate outcome.

IF YOU'VE GOT MY DOLLAR, I DON'T

THE NATURE OF COMPETITION

Know Yourself

This book contains very specific actions you and other African Americans can take to change your economic position. When devising strategies, the more you know and understand about yourself and other African Americans, the more capable you are of developing strategies that make the most of your strengths and conceal your weaknesses. The following beliefs, weaknesses, and strengths currently characterize the African-American community:

- **African Americans cannot progress without a leader to forward the cause.** Change does not require a leader, but it does require a critical mass. We need enough people who, together, form a loud enough voice to bring about change. When it comes to effecting change in a school district, for example, critical mass may consist of 30 parents. With respect to unfair contracting practices by a governmental entity, a critical mass may require at least 200 activists. Critical mass varies, depending upon what you are trying to accomplish and the entity you are confronting.

- **The problem is too big to fix: "It will never change."** Who would have thought apartheid would end so abruptly in South Africa, leaving behind a Black African president? Since 1969, man has gone to the moon, commercial airplanes have catapulted to supersonic speed, and computers and the Internet have revolutionized the world. All this progress has occurred while America has supposedly tried, unsuccessfully, to substantially improve the condition of African Americans. America accomplishes whatever it wills.

THE NATURE OF COMPETITION

Know Yourself—Self-defeating Beliefs

African Americans must not conclude that our problems are unsolvable simply because America has not "willed" a change in our community.

■ **Black folks can't come together.** This is perhaps the greatest fallacy in the African-American community. African-American fraternities and sororities, the Masons, the Eastern Star, and other long-standing African-American groups are among the most cohesive groups in America. The belief that "Black folks can't work together" is largely a media phenomenon. The instant African Americans rally to protest, march, or create a blockade, the media is quick to find one lone African American who disagrees, thus emphasizing that the activist group does not express the views of *all* within the African-American community. Since such reportage gives the impression there is no cohesiveness, the activists' initiative appears to be a major debacle and a failure. So African Americans—fearful of dissension and of being associated with a failed initiative— retreat and steer clear of the effort.

Who says that all members of a racial group must agree, even on issues that affect the entire race? Whites and others openly disagree, but African Americans are expected to be monolithic, without disagreement.

IF YOU'VE GOT MY DOLLAR, I DON'T

THE NATURE OF COMPETITION

Know Yourself—Self-defeating Beliefs

Since disagreement and dissension are part of normal group dynamics, they should be expected. If the group you are affiliated with does not share your ideas and interests, form one that does. More than one group of African Americans with different views can forward a cause. It simply means that the subject of the action has to address the concerns of multiple interest groups, all of which happen to be African-American.

■ **Aspiring for money and the better things in life is an ungodly goal.** Many African-American Christians view the pursuit of wealth as a somewhat non-Christian goal. Many of the great people in the Bible, however, were endowed with great wealth, including King David, Abraham and Sarah, and Job, just to name a few. Also, the Bible contains repeated references to abundant living and financial blessings, which include not having to contemplate whether you will eat, if you can pay your bills, or how you will acquire other life essentials. Prosperity is an important part of God's perfect plan.

THE NATURE OF COMPETITION

Know Yourself—Weaknesses

- **Preferred minority syndrome.** Many African Americans need approval from competitors that surround them. Often, these African Americans compromise their convictions and integrity by colluding with hostile competitors to wrong other African Americans. These African Americans have a huge self-esteem problem and will continue to be a part of the African-American community. So develop your plans with them in mind.

- **Too consumption-oriented.** African Americans are too quick to part with their dollars. Looking wealthy is not important. Being wealthy is.

- **Quickly lose sight of relevant issues.** Too often, African Americans become entangled in things that do not move us toward our goal. For example, many African-American women were totally unaware that the African-American beauty supply industry was being methodically taken over by Korean entrepreneurs. We abandoned thriving African-American businesses to save a few dollars at the Korean store across the street. Today, Korean business owners have a near monopoly coast-to-coast on beauty supply stores that serve African Americans.

IF YOU'VE GOT MY DOLLAR, I DON'T

THE NATURE OF COMPETITION

Know Yourself—Weaknesses

- **Blind acceptance.** African Americans are too quick to accept concepts that are designed to keep them where they are. For example, most African-American business owners quickly accept the concept of minority participation. Have you ever heard the term *majority participation*? Of course not. The assumption is that African Americans will participate and others will own the pie.

- **Double standards.** African Americans themselves are sometimes guilty of a double standard. Some continue to patronize establishments that treat them with disrespect and major store chains where security follows them around. Yet expose an African American to one bad experience with an African-American business, and all remaining African-American businesses are held responsible.

- **Relaxed standards.** Our community tolerates what no community should, such as substandard schools, substandard treatment, and even substandard music lyrics, riddled with demeaning comments about African-American men and women. We must have one standard—*excellence*—that we demand from everyone. Only then will we experience the rewards that excellence brings.

THE NATURE OF COMPETITION

Know Yourself—Strengths

- **Prominence of the Church.** African-American churches have long served as the foundation of the African-American community. Churches are the meeting places where a great number of African Americans refuel their souls to endure the difficulty of competing in America. Too many churches today, however, function as major economic entities that exist solely to create wealth for ministers and their families. At the same time, the elderly remain poor, the homeless go unserved, and children go hungry. While God desires for ministers and their families to be blessed abundantly, the church can rise and assume greater responsibility for the financial, spiritual, and emotional well-being of the African-American community by demonstrating its commitment to biblical principles and a love for people by sharing and caring: "'I will set up shepherds over them who will feed them; and they shall fear no more, nor be dismayed, nor shall they be lacking,' says the LORD." (*Jeremiah* 23:4.)

- **Fierce competitors.** African Americans are fierce competitors. Equipped with the right information and tools, more African Americans will transfer their competitive skills to the business sector, becoming formidable players in the economic arena.

IF YOU'VE GOT MY DOLLAR, I DON'T

THE NATURE OF COMPETITION

Know Yourself—Strengths

■ **African Americans are trendsetters.** We are a colorful people with incredible social influence. Ethnic groups worldwide emulate African-American styles and trends. More African Americans must learn to translate their trendsetting style and ability into wealth.

■ **Substantial resources.** Collectively, African Americans spend billions of dollars annually. That is why almost every new group that comes to America locates its businesses in the African-American community. Many competitors have profited from the many dollars spent by African Americans. In recent years, many Arabic immigrants purchased stores and businesses in the African-American community. The Asian community is also thriving on dollars spent by African Americans. Just about anyone seeking wealth—and that includes drug dealers—targets the African-American community because many of our members exercise little financial discipline and are too quick to part with their dollars. As a result, our community serves as waiting prey for any group seeking to begin its financial climb up America's economic ladder. By learning how to withhold our financial resources to coerce change, African Americans can transform America into an "African-American-friendly" society in short time.

THE NATURE OF COMPETITION

Know Yourself—Strengths

- **Collective disgust.** Collective disgust with "separate but equal" policies in the 1950s and '60s reignited the civil rights movement. While African Americans are still outraged by the disparity that characterizes our daily life, we have grown somewhat complacent, believing that the problem is too deeply rooted to correct. The collective disgust African Americans share is a powerful advocacy force waiting to be unleashed.

- **Resilience.** Historically, African Americans have excelled amid the most adverse odds, demonstrating their ability to transform adversity into triumph.

IF YOU'VE GOT MY DOLLAR, I DON'T

THE NATURE OF COMPETITION

Know Your Competitors—Strengths and Weaknesses

In addition to examining yourself, you must also scrutinize competitors' strengths and weaknesses. Make it your business to know all there is to know about your competitors. Discover how your competitors think by evaluating their strategies. Use what you learn to your advantage when developing strategies and tactics. The following are some of your competitors' strengths and weaknesses.

- **Competitors have hinged their continued economic prominence on African-American disadvantagedness.** White privilege has a cost, and the cost is Black disadvantagedness. The disadvantaged status of African Americans allows competitors to partake of financial opportunities that would otherwise be enjoyed by African Americans. African Americans will disarm competitors when they begin operating more strategically with their finances.

- **Advance knowledge.** Many competitors know about major strategic deals—such as new mall openings, neighborhood revitalization, and other important deals—long before the general public knows. Key decision-makers "sitting at the table" disseminate this information informally and in "muted voice" to a select network of associates and friends. This insider knowledge allows competitors with the required financial resources to consistently position themselves for opportunities to make even more wealth.

THE NATURE OF COMPETITION

Know Your Competitors—Strengths and Weaknesses

- **Unspoken rules.** Many groups have a clear set of unspoken rules that a majority of its members embrace, such as giving preference to persons of their race when it comes to jobs and business opportunities. In fact, some business owners offer special discounts to other business owners of the same race or ethnic origin, even though such practices are illegal.

- **Manage groups for economic betterment.** Most competitor groups exist with one purpose in mind: to create and increase wealth. They have a plan—and they all know and understand the plan. Although African-American groups share strong bonds and ties, many are largely social.

- **Control.** Even competitors who do not have substantial wealth help account for the current distribution of wealth. Many competitors occupy important positions (such as contracting officers, corporate managers and supervisors, and city buyers), and they determine who gets contracts and jobs—and who does not. Many of these decision-makers embrace the prefer-your-own mentality and thus route opportunities to members of their race.

- **Strong knowledge of their competitors' habits.** Competitors know African-American consumption habits, vulnerabilities, and needs. They have profited from understanding African-American culture and from knowing what motivates African Americans.

THE NATURE OF COMPETITION

Know Your Competitors—Strengths and Weaknesses

■ **Wealth to invest.** Because they have financial wealth and can quickly secure loans, competitors can seize opportunities at critical junctures and thus substantially increase their overall wealth.

■ **Keen knowledge of financial systems.** Competitors designed our current system of economics. They know how to use bonds, Tax Incremental Financing (TIF), and other financial instruments to accomplish major tasks. If African Americans are to compete effectively, we too must learn to identify the various financial instruments, understand their use, and know their benefits and drawbacks.

■ **Focus.** Competitors never lose focus of their goals or financial interests. And while they may disagree vehemently over tactics and approaches, they seem never to let emotions and personal feelings overshadow sound business judgment. Because African Americans have been mistreated and abused for so long, they harbor many emotions. To be effective competitors, African Americans must not act on emotions alone. Instead, African Americans must see each issue for its *financial relevancy* and seek the resolution that has a favorable financial outcome.

THE NATURE OF COMPETITION

Know Your Competitors—Strengths and Weaknesses

■ **Leverage African-American disunity.** For decades, competitors have relied upon African Americans to sabotage and stunt the progress of other African Americans. Competitors know how to leverage the *preferred minority syndrome* (page 20) to enlist African Americans in their wrongful acts. Just as African-American slave drivers—hoping to earn their masters' favor—revealed plots by other slaves to escape or mount rebellion, there are still African Americans who collude with competitors to wrong other African Americans, with the hope of becoming the "preferred minority."

Taking Control

PREPARE YOUR MIND

"Progress always involves risk; you can't steal second base and keep your foot on first."

Frederick Wilcox

TAKING CONTROL

Responsibility for Past Actions: Competitors

To compete effectively, you must feel empowered—knowing you can win the race. As an empowered African American, you must assume complete responsibility for your future, while requiring competitors to accept responsibility for past actions.

Responsibility for past actions. While Americans comprehend the horror of the Holocaust and understand why Jews are justified in combing the globe to punish those that killed, maimed, and enslaved their families, they cannot understand why African Americans simply cannot get past their experience of slavery and discrimination. The Holocaust is numbing, and so is the African-American experience:

- It is estimated that more than 5.7 million Jews died in the Holocaust; by 1860, accounts indicate that America had enslaved more than 4 million African Americans who endured the harshest of human conditions.

- The Holocaust—one in a long line of persecutions against the Jews—lasted 12 years; the legal enslavement of African Americans lasted for over two centuries.

Let's face it: Slavery is America's Holocaust. Countless African-American families were separated and destroyed; women were raped; men were castrated; children were sold as chattel; and fathers, sons, and husbands were hanged as White families and their children looked on, regarding the spectacle as a form of entertainment. While the Jewish community conducts an unprecedented and unrelenting search to find and hold accountable those who abused its people, profited at their expense during the Holocaust, or possess even a small relic

IF YOU'VE GOT MY DOLLAR, I DON'T

TAKING CONTROL

Responsibility for Past Actions: Competitors

that belonged to a Jew before the Holocaust, African Americans are expected to "just get over it."

Like the Japanese—who received payment from the U.S. government for being incarcerated in internment camps during World War II—and the Jews in their worldwide quest for recompense, African Americans must seek restitution. We must seek redress from the U.S. government that allowed the emasculation of our people and from others who advanced at our expense, including the families of plantation owners and the companies that benefitted from slavery, such as tobacco and cotton companies. We, like the Jews, must seek restitution for the pain, suffering, and deaths our families have endured. We must help America understand that affirmative action, set-asides, and other highly contested special programs are not handouts whose merits require debate. They are entitlements—partial recompense for social crimes committed repeatedly against our families. The American legal system gives us certain rights. We must exercise our right to be made whole.

TAKING CONTROL

Responsibility for the Future: African Americans

While the African-American past is characterized by slavery, discrimination, and unfair treatment, empowered African Americans accept complete responsibility for their future.

Responsibility for our future. Some things *are* Black and White. As much as we resent being categorized into groups, the reality is that groupings are very useful. Scientists use groupings to categorize similar beings; mathematicians use groupings for problem-solving and identifying patterns; and the business world categorizes industries, stocks, and target markets by groups. Groupings are necessary because they make information manageable and analysis possible, especially when topics are complex.

We both embrace and reject the use of groupings when it comes to race. When a report or an allegation is negative, we quickly emphasize that we are not responsible for the actions of others in our group. To paraphrase Dr. Martin Luther King, Jr., just slightly, "We want to be judged by the content of our character and not by the color of our skin." When the label or perception assigned to our group is considered complimentary by African Americans, such as the often proclaimed sexual prowess of African-American males, we seldom complain that we are being viewed as a group.

Like it or not, the actions of a critical mass define how a race is perceived. As African Americans, we must accept responsibility for the negative perceptions associated with our race, just as White America must accept responsibility for the perception that it is racist and unfair. The future of African Americans is yours to define.

IF YOU'VE GOT MY DOLLAR, I DON'T

TAKING CONTROL

Responsibility for the Future: African Americans

Prepare for competition. Just as an athlete spends enormous time and energy preparing for competition, so must you.

- **Develop a voracious appetite for information.** Read. Stay abreast of current events. Learn all you can about issues that affect you. Discover how high finance works, including the importance of saving and financial planning. Study the various financial instruments, the benefits they offer, and the ways they work. Understand the importance of life insurance, wills, and trusts, as well as the unique benefits each offers. Also learn about other instruments competitors use to create wealth in their businesses and personal lives.

- **Practice critical thinking.** View issues from many perspectives, not just your own. Read to identify different viewpoints and opinions. Discuss your thoughts with others, listening attentively to their ideas and perspectives. Diversity of opinion and thought helps you make informed decisions about crucial matters.

- **Master the tools of competition.** Language—both written and spoken—is perhaps the most important skill needed to compete effectively. With language people communicate their opinions, form alliances with others who share their interests and concerns, devise plans, communicate their position, and bring attention to what concerns them. In the arena of economic competition, the ability to communicate effectively is your most important weapon. Learn to write skillfully and verbalize your ideas, with clarity and strength. Never harass another African American for enunciating clearly and speaking effectively. To speak properly is not "talking White."

NOTES

Creating Wealth

PREPARE YOUR MIND

"To turn $100 into $110 is work. To turn $100 million into $110 million is inevitable."

Edgar Bronfman

CREATING WEALTH

Acquisition, Retention, and Extraction (ARE)

Why is amassing substantial wealth important for the African-American community? African Americans have more health problems, lower educational achievement, and even a shorter life span than most competitors do. Why? Because for centuries, African Americans have lived *without* the benefits and choices that wealth brings. Since wealth can improve quality of life and, consequently, the emotional and physical well-being of countless African Americans, increasing wealth in the African-American community is not an option. It is an imperative.

What is wealth? Wealth is a picture of your net worth. Net worth is determined by totaling the things you own that have a financial value (home, business, stocks, bonds, etc.) and then subtracting all amounts you owe (liabilities).

How are African Americans faring in the wealth category? According to Melvin L. Oliver and Thomas M. Shapiro in *Black Wealth/White Wealth: A New Perspective on Racial Inequality*, "Whites possess nearly twelve times as much median net worth as blacks." This wealth disparity is not attributable to poor planning on the part of African Americans and excellent planning by Whites. Instead, this disparity is *a numerical representation of the benefits that generations of White privilege bring.* By mastering the financial principles known to competitors for generations, African Americans can significantly increase their wealth.

CREATING WEALTH

Acquisition, Retention, and Extraction (ARE)

How does wealth occur? Wealth is a function of ARE: Acquisition, Retention, and Extraction.

■ **Acquisition is the process of making money.** Money is legally acquired from earnings, investments, and transfer of wealth.

■ **Retention is the process of keeping and investing what you have.** You cannot participate in the wealth-creation process without retention.

■ **Extraction is the process of removing wealth from African Americans.** Extraction largely accounts for the dire financial position of many African Americans. Extraction occurs in many forms, including money spent purchasing illegal substances; money spent defending wrongful police actions; and income foregone by African Americans due to disparate employment and contracting practices. *Any disparity that costs African Americans financially is extraction.* To increase wealth, African Americans must prevent extraction.

NOTES

Increasing Acquisition

PREPARE YOUR MIND

"Small opportunities are often the beginning of great enterprises."

Demosthenes

INCREASING ACQUISITION

Acquisition—the first step in wealth creation—is the process of acquiring money from earnings, investments, and transfer of wealth.

Earnings and Investments

Few people become wealthy only from working. Most wealth results from investing, which is using money to earn more money. As such, one of the primary reasons for working is to earn money so you can save and invest. There are several factors that determine your ability to make money. They include:

- **Educational achievement that leads to professional accomplishments.**

- **Ingenuity and creativity.**

- **Learning that leads to a wealth-bearing trade.**

- **Business ownership.**

- **Partnerships and collaborations.**

IF YOU'VE GOT MY **DOLLAR**, I DON'T

INCREASING ACQUISITION

▸ **Educational achievement that leads to professional accomplishments.** Without education, professional accomplishment is extremely difficult. The economic prominence of the African-American community requires a clear, intimate understanding of the relationship between education and professional pursuits.

▸ **Ingenuity and creativity.** I know a man who supported his family by selling hangers to dry cleaners—and he supported his family very well. African Americans, particularly disadvantaged African Americans, have long been told they do not have wealth because they do not have an education. This message has caused many African Americans with low standardized test scores and low academic accomplishments to just give up. While, admittedly, a good education is invaluable, there are many competitors who are relatively uneducated, yet have made millions by responding to a need that had gone unnoticed or by coming up with a new idea altogether.

▸ **Learning that leads to a wealth-bearing trade.** If you lack a formal education, there is still a wealth of opportunities awaiting you. Embark upon a mission to determine your talents. It might be as simple as cutting and manicuring lawns; painting homes; driving a semi; cleaning carpets; or providing construction, electrical, or

INCREASING ACQUISITION

plumbing services. If formal education is not in your plan, do not give up until you find a trade that will allow you to generate income. If you need help identifying a trade that is suited to your interests and abilities, visit the local library. There are many publications listing occupations that currently exist, as well as ones for which there is growing demand. Whatever you decide, do it meticulously and with excellence, attending to every little detail. Others will soon hear of your excellent work, and they will seek your services.

▶ **Business ownership.** Business ownership can be very profitable. For most African Americans, building a business is very difficult because they must compete for opportunities long enjoyed by competitors. Also, African-American businesses encounter more disruptions, since hostile competitors in strategic positions often work vigorously to limit the businesses' progress. African Americans can ensure the preservation and growth of African-American businesses by spending at those businesses a significant portion of the estimated $400 billion African Americans spend annually. Even if you have only a few dollars to spend, make a special effort to do business with African-American firms. If a particular African-American business does not meet your needs, patronize another one that can and does.

INCREASING ACQUISITION

Do not, however, require a higher standard from African-American businesses than you would require from those of competitors. But do expect and insist on quality products and services.

▶ **Partnerships and collaborations.** African Americans must begin exploring new ways of building businesses. The current approach often does not provide the return African Americans seek. As such, more African Americans must pool resources to generate large cash amounts that enable them to pursue large-scale business ventures. Approach collaborative ventures as you would any other business activity. Seek the advice of a qualified attorney and an accounting professional when entering into partnerships or other collaborations, no matter who is involved. Scrutinize every aspect of the contractual agreement to ensure that every relevant issue pertaining to the relationship is addressed.

Transfer of Wealth

Significant acquisition occurs through transfer of wealth. Transfer of wealth occurs in many forms, such as gifts, wills, trusts, life insurance proceeds, and other types of instruments. Appropriately using estate planning instruments to transfer wealth upon death is a vital aspect of generational wealth-building.

INCREASING ACQUISITION

▶ **Life insurance.** Competitors routinely use life insurance as a means of passing wealth to the next generation. It is one practice increasing numbers of African Americans can adopt to ensure the next generation begins on a strong financial footing. There are many different types of life insurance policies; each has its own set of benefits. Do your homework and identify the plan that is best for you. In some instances, it might be worthwhile to have the beneficiary pay the life insurance premium, since he or she will ultimately benefit from the policy.

▶ **Wills, trusts, and other estate-planning instruments.** With estate planning, the ultimate goal is to ensure assets are transferred to the desired party without being diminished in value by probate and estate taxes.

There are many ways to transfer wealth and avoid probate. While they are too numerous to discuss here, reputable books and Internet sites provide detailed information about the advantages of each estate-planning option. Do your homework and get your business in order.

Strengthening Retention

African Americans will never experience financial freedom and wealth if they do not make it happen for themselves.

STRENGTHENING RETENTION

Wealth-creation Strategy

Retention is a major factor in wealth creation. It is an ongoing process that includes *saving* and *investing*. To accumulate wealth, you must save and invest a significant portion of what you earn.

- **Saving.** Saving is the first step to financial independence and stability. It takes inner strength and discipline to save. Here are some specific steps in the saving process:

  - **Decide to save.** Saving is a decision to put money aside. Saving can seem difficult when you are accustomed to buying what you want when you want it. Realize that every expenditure you make steals from you an opportunity to grow wealthy. Abandon your need to impress others with flashy jewelry, cars, and assets that might make you look prosperous when in fact you are struggling to pay the bills. Avoid the tendency to spend money on unnecessary items, such as convenience store snacks, weekly manicures, and other nonessentials. If you smoke, give it up—it's an expensive habit that robs both your health and your wallet. Deny yourself and save.

    Remember: Looking wealthy is not important. Being wealthy is.

STRENGTHENING RETENTION

Wealth-creation Strategy

Even when you begin accumulating wealth, continue to save and invest. Wealth-building is a long-term commitment. When done properly, it allows you to pass money on to your children and their children.

▸ **Be consistent.** The more you save, the more excited you will become about saving. Save even if your spouse cannot or will not join the plan to save. Involve your children in your savings plan. Teach them at an early age the value of saving, working, and investing. Help them understand how wealth is amassed. Create in your household a "spirit of saving."

▸ **Decide how much you will save.** Write the amount you are going to save on a small card. Place your card where you will see it several times a day. When deciding how much you are going to save monthly, be aggressive—but also be realistic. For you, realistic might mean personal savings worth $10. For someone else, realistic might mean $500. Whatever you decide, determine to make your goal a reality. As your savings grow, you will become more vigilant about finding additional ways to save.

▸ **Budget.** Developing a financial plan is first and foremost. Without a financial plan, your money will simply depart from you. A plan creates accountability: It makes you take notice of what you are doing with the money you earn. Even if you seldom have enough money to pay your bills, you can benefit from financial

STRENGTHENING RETENTION

Wealth-creation Strategy

planning. "Creating a Financial Plan," which begins on page 172, lists resources that will help you create a budget and manage your finances. Spend considerable time learning about money management and investing.

▸ **Make wise purchasing decisions.** Making bad purchasing decisions can negatively affect your net worth. Some assets such as property, land, and bonds grow in value. Others, like cars, decrease rapidly in value. Consider an asset's ability to hold its value when deciding how much you will spend for that asset.

▸ **Plan your next step.** If you are saving a few dollars each week, your next goal might be accumulating the minimum amount needed to open a savings account. Once you have opened a savings account, your next step might be opening an investment account. Always plan your next step, viewing it as a goal. Planning means learning more about money management and the options you have.

▸ **Reduce your debt.** If you have a lot of credit card and other debts, you will need a plan to get back on track. If things are really bad, contact Consumer Credit Counseling (or a similar nonprofit credit-counseling agency), which will work out—confidentially and free of charge—a plan that will allow you to pay creditors what you can, while helping you reestablish a favorable credit rating.

IF YOU'VE GOT MY DOLLAR, I DON'T

STRENGTHENING RETENTION

Wealth-creation Strategy

> ▶ **Practice tax avoidance.** The more taxes you pay, the less you have to save and invest. A critical part of your long-term plan to create wealth should include a tax-avoidance strategy. A good strategy helps you (1) legally put off paying taxes on investments as long as possible; (2) identify investments that will yield the most income, after taxes are paid; and (3) reduce taxes by shifting income to family members who are in lower tax brackets, such as children and the elderly.

- ■ **Investing.** If you really want to realize wealth, you must make your money work for you! Growing your money is accomplished by investing. Some wealthy competitors earn more in a day from their investments than you earn in an entire year working. Others live on their investment dividends alone.

  > ▶ **Ways to go.** If you are afraid of investing, just remember there is something for everyone. For the fearful at heart, there are conservative instruments such as low-risk mutual funds, bonds, Treasury bills (T-bills), and certificates of deposit (CDs). For the risk-taker, there are high-risk mutual funds, stocks, and other instruments that pay a higher return, though they present greater risks. Start by investing in corporate names you know are likely to continue prospering, such as General Motors, Ford Motor Company, and other successful firms. Request a prospectus to learn more about the firm and its current financial position.

STRENGTHENING RETENTION

Wealth-creation Strategy

▶ **Educate your way to wealth.** When preparing to invest, educate yourself. Do not rely solely upon someone else to manage your funds. At least be reasonably knowledgeable about the decisions being made relative to your portfolio.

There are several ways you can learn about investing. Many community colleges offer evening seminars on investing. You can also learn a lot by visiting your local library to acquire resources on investing. Another option is to form an investment club. Don't forget: The Internet is another invaluable information source. Make sure, however, to access Web sites run by reputable investment firms. If you are uncertain about a firm's reputation, consult the Better Business Bureau (BBB)— another online resource.

▶ **Money is made by consistent investing.** Avoid get-rich-quick schemes, fly-by-night scams, and even legitimate lures of instant wealth. You are not likely to win the state's lottery, so instead of buying lottery tickets, save those dollars and invest.

■ **Understand how money works.** Money is more than a consumption tool to purchase things we want. Money is the fuel that drives our economy. It is therefore important that you understand how money works:

IF YOU'VE GOT MY DOLLAR, I DON'T

STRENGTHENING RETENTION

Wealth-creation Strategy

▶ **Multiplier effect.** Money has a multiplier effect because every dollar spent generates wealth for numerous people. For example, let's assume you buy a car for $500. The $500 car cost the dealer only $450, so the dealer can use the $50 profit toward the purchase of another car. The dealer also earns money each time you visit the dealership for repairs or maintenance. The finance company earns interest from the $500 it loaned you. Gasoline companies benefit financially from your repeat purchases of gas. Thus, every dollar spent multiplies, creating income for numerous people and businesses in the supply chain.

▶ **Compounding.** Compounding is the interest paid on both the *principal* (amount you invest) and the *accrued interest* (interest your investment has already earned). Compounding causes your investments to grow.

Let's assume you invest $100 a month for 30 years at a 10 percent interest rate. Let's also assume that interest has been applied monthly to principal and accumulated interest. Your total investment of $36,000—$100 a month over a period of 30 years (360 months)—will grow to $226,049 due to the miracle of compound interest!

The Physics *of* Money

STRENGTHENING RETENTION

Wealth-creation Strategy

Years	Compounding	Return
10	Monthly at 10 percent	$ 20,485
20	Monthly at 10 percent	$ 75,937
30	Monthly at 10 percent	$226,049

Thus, if you are a lender or investor, compounding works for you, causing an amount you invested or loaned to multiply. (Note, however, that if you are a borrower, compounding works against you because you have to repay substantially more than you borrowed.)

When compounding and the multiplier effect of money are considered, the economic power of the over $400 billion that African Americans spend annually becomes quite apparent.

Harness your power: *Earn more, save more, and invest more.*

Preventing Extraction

Only African Americans know what it is like to be Black in America. Disparate treatment is an ever-present reality that invades your life like a burglar, stealing from you opportunity, equity, and any vestige of fair play. For this crime, there are no safe places, no bandages, no healing of the wounds. There are few politicians to protect your interests and no laws that effectively shield you from disparity's constant barrage. You are an African American in America. You are alone. America knows it and so do you.

PREVENTING EXTRACTION

Extraction depletes the African-American community financially. Extraction takes several forms, including:

- Reduced income potential resulting from inadequate education or denied learning opportunities.

- Discriminatory practices that prevent African Americans from advancing in the business arena.

- Illegal activities that divert African-American dollars to competitors such as drug traffickers.

- Race-related criminal justice actions that wrongfully entangle African Americans in the criminal justice system.

- Lending practices that wrongly deny African Americans capital needed to acquire homes, businesses, and other wealth-generating assets.

To prevent extraction, African Americans must:

1. Uncover and eliminate processes that prevent African Americans from amassing substantial wealth.

2. Develop and implement Action Plans to correct process inequities.

3. Remain vigilant.

4. Participate in the rule-making process.

Sharpening Your Focus: Uncover Unfair Processes

PREPARE YOUR MIND

"No problem can stand the assault of sustained thinking."

Voltaire

PREVENTING EXTRACTION

Sharpening Your Focus: Uncover Unfair Processes

African Americans must actively work to uncover processes that place them at a disadvantage when it comes to creating wealth. A personal event, casual research, or a news report can raise your suspicions that you and other African Americans are *not* being treated fairly. While you might have an idea that a problem exists, you will want to confirm your suspicions with objective data. When possible, acquire race-based data that shows how African Americans are succeeding in comparison to competitors. Often, you will find that no race-based data exists on the subject. This lack of data often occurs by design, allowing your competitors to disguise how poorly African Americans are doing relative to competitors.

Once you have reasonably concluded a problem exists, study the problem further to uncover the source of the problem, as well as the social dynamics, laws, practices, and policies that allow the problem to persist.

ocesses

is unfair, determine if
the process is

ou believe to be unfair.
ents such as
ters, regulations, and
umentation containing
e problem. If a
ow the process should
ntity to develop one.
rmulating policy.

e valid. Verify that the
s. For example, in
otion practices within
munications company, a
h me the company's
. The formula relied
African Americans
ted, I pointed out that
the underrepresentation
upper management.
ppear to be fair, the
patterns of disparity.

PREVENTING EXTRACTION

Sharpening Your Focus: Uncover Unfair Processes

- **Verify that the process is being administered fairly.** In order to show preference, many hostile competitors violate established rules. So make sure processes that have economic outcomes are followed to the letter. If the process is not followed, insist that the party repeat the process, abiding by the rules. Do not accept a promise of "we will do it right the next time." Your opportunity for economic advancement is **now**. So insist on **now**.

- **Confirm that the outcome is fair.** Verify that objective data confirm that the outcome is proper and fair. Often, decision-makers will follow the process but will dismiss the outcome in favor of one that agrees with their preference.

Planning

In competition, success doesn't just happen. It is planned, every step of the way.

PREVENTING EXTRACTION

Create an Action Plan

Once you have analyzed information and determined that a problem exists, you can prepare an *Action Plan* to correct the problem. Every *Action Plan*, at minimum, should include:

1. A *Problem Statement* describing the problem in detail and the solution.

2. An *Advocacy Plan* outlining steps your group must take to resolve the problem.

IF YOU'VE GOT MY DOLLAR, I DON'T

PREVENTING EXTRACTION

Action Plan: Create a Problem Statement

The problem statement should clearly define the problem and the outcome you are seeking. When developing your problem statement, define:

- **The problem.**

- **How the problem affects the African-American community.**

- **What happens if the problem is not addressed.**

- **The proposed solution.** The solution is a summary of principle outcomes needed to correct an unfair process or practice. While the solution should always be equitable, it does not necessarily have to apply to competitors. An equitable solution may involve preferences and other special rules that are designed to allow African Americans who were only recently allowed to join the competition an opportunity to catch up with competitors. Affirmative action programs, for example, are often said to be unfair because they give African Americans preference. The preference these programs offer is designed to offset the preference competitors have enjoyed for centuries.

For example, a problem statement related to unarmed African-American males being shot or otherwise killed by police officers might read as follows:

PREVENTING EXTRACTION

Action Plan: Create a Problem Statement

The Problem

There are too many killings of unarmed African-American males by police that go unpunished.

The Effect

Too many African American males are dying needlessly, leaving behind fatherless children, grieving families, and a demoralized community.

What Happens If the Problem Is Not Addressed

Killing of African Americans by police will become increasingly commonplace.

The Solution

Enact legislation that makes "accidental killings" by police a federal offense that automatically commands a specified number of years' imprisonment, removal from the police force, and the relinquishing of retirement benefits.

PREVENTING EXTRACTION

Action Plan: Create an Advocacy Plan

Once you have defined the problem statement, the next step is developing an *advocacy plan*. Advocacy is the process of convincing others to support, endorse, and forward issues that concern you. The plan is your road map, outlining step-by-step actions you must take to realize the solution.

The advocacy plan is absolutely crucial and will largely determine the success of your effort. At minimum, your advocacy plan should specify:

- **Who will head the effort.**
- **Who has jurisdiction over the issue.**
- **How you will galvanize support.**
- **How you will bring the advocacy effort to a successful conclusion.**
- **A timeline for accomplishing your goals.**

PREVENTING EXTRACTION

Action Plan: Create an Advocacy Plan

The goal of your advocacy plan is to create enough support for the issue that politicians will consider remedying the problem a national priority. The following is a more detailed explanation of an advocacy plan.

- **Who will head the effort.** If the problem you are working to abolish affects African Americans nationwide—such as police killings of unarmed African-American males—enlist the assistance of a national organization or create a national nonprofit organization solely for the purpose of accomplishing your goal.

- **Who has jurisdiction over the issue.** Knowing who has jurisdiction and control may help you determine where to direct your advocacy efforts—but not always. National legislation might be the only way to resolve a problem that falls under state or local control, such as police killings of unarmed African Americans.

IF YOU'VE GOT MY DOLLAR, I DON'T

PREVENTING EXTRACTION

Action Plan: Create an Advocacy Plan

- **How you will galvanize support (advocacy).** To be effective, you must have at least one of the following: (1) *Political clout and strong affiliations*; (2) *active involvement of a critical mass*; and (3) *substantial dollars to persuade and heighten awareness of the advocate's position*. The more elements you enlist, the more likely your effort is to succeed.

  ▶ **Political clout and strong affiliations.** Strong leaders and organizations bring instant attention to systemic injustices. They use their political ties to quickly broker solutions. Leaders are generally more willing to get involved when an issue has widespread support.

  ▶ **Active involvement of a critical mass.** Large numbers of people united in a cause speak volumes. Develop a communications plan that enlists widespread sustained support for your issue. Make sure your communications plan specifies:

  (a) The groups you will target and the key messages you will communicate. Messages should promote your cause, enlist support, and combat objections or attacks opponents are likely to unleash. In the effort to stop police from shooting unarmed African Americans, you will want to target:

PREVENTING EXTRACTION

Action Plan: Create an Advocacy Plan

- **Community at large:** Portray, numerically, how often unarmed African Americans are shot by police in comparison to those of other races.

- **Politicians:** Make politicians understand that African Americans will no longer tolerate African Americans being gunned down by police without provocation or cause.

- **African-American community:** Help African Americans realize that temporary outbursts expressing displeasure with police-alleged accidental killings will not accomplish change. Correcting the problem will require *prolonged, sustained advocacy*.

(b) How you will deliver your messages (television, radio, etc.). Will your group use television advertising? Newspapers? The Internet? Newsletters? Bulletins? Continually devise fresh new approaches and versions of each message to maintain media and public interest.

(c) How frequently you will communicate with each target group. Make a decision about the frequency of communications. Increase or decrease the frequency to achieve desired results.

PREVENTING EXTRACTION

Action Plan: Create an Advocacy Plan

(d) Tactics you will use. Tactics your group employs must make a compelling argument for change, encouraging prompt resolution. Tactics may range from financial boycotts to sit-ins, blockades, marches, and any other effective action you can imagine. With regard to police shootings of unarmed African Americans, for example, African Americans should have carriage- or wagon-drawn funeral processions down city main streets during rush hour each time an unarmed African American is killed. The sheer frequency with which these processions occur will emphasize the need for change.

▶ **Substantial dollars to persuade and heighten awareness of the advocates' position.** Money—the third tool of advocacy—provides immeasurable returns. With money, you can back and promote candidates; hire lobbyists to work full-time on forwarding specific issues; and fund other efforts related to your cause. With regard to raising funds:

   ▪ **Decide how and where you will solicit funds.** You can target ethical competitors who endorse change; churches; and various African-American groups, including fraternities and sororities. You can also sponsor fundraisers such as walk-a-thons, dance-a-thons, talent shows, auctions, garage sales, and book fairs.

PREVENTING EXTRACTION

Action Plan: Create an Advocacy Plan

- **Develop a budget**. The budget should detail how much you need to fund each aspect of your effort.

- **Install financial controls.** Funds mismanagement can kill an effort. Secure a certified public accountant (CPA) and install controls to ensure proper accounting of all funds.

■ **How you will assess the effort.** Assess the effectiveness of your effort, every step of the way. Set goals before you begin a tactical effort. When the effort is complete, evaluate your effectiveness. Use what you learn when planning your next effort.

■ **How you will bring the advocacy effort to conclusion.** Your advocacy plan should also define what your group will compromise and what it will not. Do not compromise process equity, since your goal is to ensure that you and competitors are operating by the same rules. Select skilled negotiators who know the group's position and are capable of strategically negotiating the issue to conclusion.

■ **A timeline for accomplishing your goal.** Proceed according to a timeline. Adhering to a timeline will help keep your effort on track.

Improving Processes

PREPARE YOUR MIND

"Where we cannot invent, we may at least improve."

Charles Caleb Colton

PREVENTING EXTRACTION

Improving Processes

Because there are thousands of injustices African Americans can tackle, we often become entangled in struggles that do not move us toward our goal of financial prosperity; they simply make us feel better. Empowered Africans Americans devote their energies and resources to improving processes that allow them to compete on equal footing with competitors. Such processes include:

- **Educational processes** that produce financial rewards in the long term and help place your child at the head of the pack. Such processes include program development, school maintenance and construction, school governance, and faculty selection.

- **Business processes** that produce immediate financial returns, such as contracting, hiring, and promotions.

- **Criminal justice processes** that wrongfully incarcerate African Americans, stealing their income-generating capacity as well as prime years of their lives.

- **Legal processes** that deny African Americans recompense and monetary judgements they rightfully deserve.

- **Other processes** that give competitors unfair advantage.

IF YOU'VE GOT MY DOLLAR, I DON'T

PREVENTING EXTRACTION

Schools and Education

Education empowers! It is the primary means by which we gain knowledge. Education gives context to life. It helps us reason and problem-solve our way to desired goals and outcomes. It also increases our ability to generate income. The current education system simply does not deliver for African Americans and, as a result, extracts enormous wealth from the African-American community.

The following reprint from the March 1, 2000, *USA Today*, written by Tamara Henry, vividly portrays how African Americans and other minorities are faring in the American educational system.

Report: Education not equal yet

Forty-six years after the Supreme Court's *Brown v. Board of Education* decision ended school segregation, public schools still fail to provide minorities the same quality of education as they do white students, a report released today says.

The Applied Research Center, based in Oakland, Calif., says minority students are placed at a serious disadvantage on every key indicator studied at a dozen U.S. school districts last year. For example:

▶ Black, Hispanic and Native American students are suspended or expelled in numbers disproportionate to those of whites. Expulsion and suspensions of Hispanics in Salem, Ore., and Durham, N.C., were two to four times as high as their proportion of the pupil population.

Continued on next page

PREVENTING EXTRACTION

Schools and Education

> ▶ Minority students have less access to advanced and gifted programs. In Los Angeles, 8% of advanced-placement participants are black and 44% are Latino, although they represent 14% and 69% of the school population. White students make up 11% of the population and 23% of advanced-placement classes.
>
> ▶ The racial makeup of a teaching corps rarely catches that of the student body.
>
> "The inequality amounts to a deep pattern of institutional racism," says report co-author Libero Della Piana.
>
> However, Ward Connerly, who worked to dismantle affirmative action in California, says, "You cannot conclude that this is a race-based problem." He points to the stellar academic achievements of Asian students who attend the same schools as other minorities.
>
> Some conservatives say that evidence of inequalities is irrelevant without proof of intent. But Della Piana says, "Without knowing the racial breakdown and racial disparities, it's impossible to come up with policies that address those gaps."
>
> Copyright 2000, USA TODAY. Reprinted with permission.

IF YOU'VE GOT MY DOLLAR, I DON'T

PREVENTING EXTRACTION

Schools and Education

African Americans must have at their command all the intellectual prowess and fortitude a community of people can muster in order to race ahead of competitors. We require smart, clear thinkers and excellent problem-solvers—proactive people who, regardless of their station in life, are willing to read and learn everything there is to know about America's systems. As such, African Americans must reevaluate every aspect of education—from the *way* it is delivered, to *where* it is delivered, to *how* it is delivered. In fact, African Americans should convene a "think tank" devoted solely to exploring how schools can use technology and other tools to enhance learning and skill development.

We must also help our children appreciate education and pursue it with commitment and vigor. Some actions African Americans can take to improve the quality of education are:

- **Involve interested third parties.** View issues not only as they affect you and your children but also as they affect the larger community. When it comes to schools, do not confine yourself to your neighborhood, since the people who need help the most are least prepared to effect change. Many disadvantaged African-American communities have school systems that could benefit from the involvement of interested third parties.

PREVENTING EXTRACTION

Schools and Education

- **Extend school days.** Secure data, by race and grade, detailing how students are performing relative to competitors' children. Students in predominantly African-American schools that have test scores lower than the national average should be required to attend school for extended hours and during the summer, if necessary. This added time will allow educators to develop the math, grammar, and writing skills not previously instilled.

- **Employ consultants.** School systems can supplement classes with programs and instruction provided by consultants who possess specialized skills in the areas of writing, grammar, speaking, and math. Most training consultants know how to make learning interesting, enjoyable, and effective.

- **Make extra enrichment available to all students.** Know all there is to know about the enrichment programs in your school district. You might be surprised to discover there are a disproportionate number of competitor children in gifted programs and a disproportionate number of African-American children in remedial and learning disabled programs, even when the school district has a near equal representation of African Americans and competitors.

  Rather than separating "gifted" students, promote in-class enrichment so that all children are privy to high-quality learning experiences. If the gifted program is guided by state-mandated criteria, address the problem at the state

PREVENTING EXTRACTION

Schools and Education

level and **change the criteria**. Do whatever it takes to ensure that your child is also privy to extra enrichment and any quality learning experiences competitors' children enjoy.

- **Ensure funding parity.** For over a century, schools in predominantly African-American districts have been grossly underfunded. Some school districts derive most of their funding from the municipality's tax base. Such formulas leave African-American schools understaffed, without technology, and operating with mere basics—or less.

  First, determine how your school is funded. Does the formula used to fund schools account for students and schools in more affluent areas having better facilities, technology, and curricula than schools in predominantly African-American communities? Whatever funding formula is causing the disparity, insist on change and be vigilant. Expect that your competitors will wage an all-out fight when it comes to education, since it has been one of the primary tools competitors have used to give their children a competitive advantage. Insist that your state government and the federal government make schools in African-American communities comparable in every way— *particularly as it relates to results*—no matter what it costs. **Make your position clear: Unequal education, for whatever reason, is no longer tolerable!**

PREVENTING EXTRACTION

Schools and Education

- **Introduce school Board of Trustees.** For each public school, appoint a Board of Trustees to oversee school governance. Trustees would have latitude to implement programs and policies that contribute to the financial and academic betterment of the school, as long as such efforts do not conflict with district school policy.

- **Monitor school facilities.** Require school districts to submit annual inventory listings identifying the physical components of a school, including physical assets; structural dimensions, such as pool size and gymnasium size; and the depreciated and nondepreciated value of assets and structures. Inventory listings would allow for school facilities in competitors' neighborhoods to be compared to those found in predominantly African-American communities.

- **Teacher/student ratios.** Compare the teacher/student ratio at predominantly African-American schools to those in competitor neighborhoods. A lower student/teacher ratio allows for more individualized attention and instruction.

- **Conduct teacher assessments.** Test teachers to determine their abilities and shortcomings. Compare teacher preparedness in competitor school districts to that of teachers in predominantly African-American school districts. Determine if teacher deficiencies are being transferred to students. Take corrective action to ensure all teachers are equipped to provide first-quality education to all students.

IF YOU'VE GOT MY DOLLAR, I DON'T

PREVENTING EXTRACTION

Schools and Education

- **More demanding standards.** Even in a time when African Americans were denied every available resource, there were extremely accomplished and notable African-American scholars, such as Frederick Douglass, who understood the vital importance of stretching their minds by reading, contemplating ideas, learning, and exploring possibilities. As a community, African Americans must implant in the minds of our children, at the *earliest age*, the expectation that they will *excel academically*, complete high school, go to college, and become productive and strategic members of our society. In addition to establishing high academic expectations, we must also examine school curricula and instruction to ensure our youth are challenged in a most vigorous manner, academically.

- **More learning.** Have you noticed that most community programs for African-American youth are generally of a social nature? It is assumed that to attract and retain the attention of African-American youth—particularly males—you need basketball. While basketball and other sports enhance quality of life, it sometimes seems African Americans have morning basketball, afternoon basketball, evening basketball, and even midnight basketball. Replace some of the sports activities with morning technology, afternoon technology, evening technology, and midnight technology.

PREVENTING EXTRACTION

Employment

While some corporations have African Americans represented at every level, others have a few African Americans in prominent positions to give the impression that the corporation is one that readily and fairly promotes African Americans. A closer look, however, reveals organizations where African Americans are overlooked when promotions and opportunities become available. A significant number of African Americans working together can change the employment practices of major corporations overnight. Here are some of the actions African Americans can take or encourage:

■ **Withhold finances to force change.** Respond to organizations' and leaders' calls for financial boycotts and do it with complete resolve—even if it requires significant sacrifice. Be willing to discipline yourself and to forego spending your money when a boycott is underway. Expect that the media will be there to gauge the strength and effectiveness of the boycott. You might be tempted to think that your one purchase will not make a difference. Wrong! Every dollar counts in economic competition. **Withholding your money will make a difference**, since most businesses—including large businesses—cannot operate without cash flow for long periods of time. When a leader or organization calls for a national boycott, withhold your dollars as long as the business is willing to withhold its opportunities. You will soon discover just how powerful your dollars are.

PREVENTING EXTRACTION

Employment

- **Implement hassle-free system for addressing discrimination.**
  African Americans do business with major corporations
  nationwide. We purchase beer from Anheuser-Busch,
  Coors, and Miller; we buy food from Procter & Gamble
  and Kraft; we rent cars from Hertz, Enterprise, Budget, and
  Alamo; we buy cars and automobiles from General Motors,
  Ford, and DaimlerChrysler—the list goes on and on.
  Corporations seeking the patronage of the African-
  American community should agree to allow a third party—
  selected and hired by a minority-sensitive organization—to
  arbitrate employment discrimination complaints speedily
  and at no cost to the corporation's employees. Corporations
  should agree to abide by arbitration findings.

- **Revamp Equal Employment Opportunity Commission (EEOC) laws.**
  Most African Americans are not aware you cannot sue for
  employment discrimination until EEOC authorizes you to
  do so. This process, which involves petitioning EEOC for a
  notice of right to sue, requires African Americans to exhaust
  EEOC administrative procedures before they can bring a
  discrimination action before the courts. Additionally, EEOC
  limits the total amount employees can recoup for both
  punitive and compensatory damages to $300,000 for the
  largest employers. For smaller employers, the caps are less.
  Although persons bringing discrimination lawsuits may
  recoup lost wages, benefits, attorney fees, and other similar

PREVENTING EXTRACTION

Employment

claims—in addition to compensatory and punitive damages—the caps nevertheless discourage discrimination lawsuits. Attorneys, aware that legal fees can easily exceed the amount awarded a plaintiff, often refuse to take such cases on a contingent-fee basis. As such, African Americans should seek to change deficient civil rights legislation, including removing damage caps and abolishing the right to sue process. If companies were subject to greater loss, they would work harder to ensure their environments are free from discriminatory activity. (**Note:** The right to sue process and damage caps also govern sex discrimination, reverse discrimination, and most other EEOC-related complaints.)

■ **Mandate that companies publish employment and staff statistics.** Most employers must report employment data to EEOC, as prescribed by Title VII of the 1964 Civil Rights Act. The act, however, prevents EEOC from publishing company-specific employment statistics. Since congressional leaders, the President, and the judiciary take an oath to uphold the Constitution, they have a legal responsibility to implement laws and processes that ensure African Americans are privy to the same constitutional guarantees others enjoy. Thus, Congress should require that companies make their employment data public, including:

IF YOU'VE GOT MY DOLLAR, I DON'T

PREVENTING EXTRACTION

Employment

> ▸ Employment data by race, sex, ethnic origin, and occupation.

> ▸ Salary listing that details the ethnicity, tenure, sex, and compensation of each employee in the job group. This listing will enable African Americans to monitor for equal pay since, historically, companies have paid White workers more than their African-American counterparts.

> ▸ Number of demotions, by race.

> ▸ Statistics on terminations, by race.

> ▸ Statistics on disciplinary actions, by race.

> ▸ Other data warranted.

- ◾ **Revise federal government EEOC process.** The federal government's EEOC process is quite different from that of the private sector. Even so, the federal government should lead the way when it comes to abolishing employment discrimination. It should afford those injured by discrimination an opportunity to recover punitive damages, which it currently does not allow. It should also require the immediate dismissal of any federal employee who engages in discriminatory practices.

PREVENTING EXTRACTION

Private-sector Contracting

Business is a fierce competitive arena, since it is where much wealth can be obtained in a short period of time. African-American entrepreneurs are forced to survive while competitor businesses are allowed to thrive. Like competitors, African Americans must compete vigorously for dollars spent in the business arena. The following is a specific initiative African Americans can pursue:

■ **Minority vendor programs that work.** Most minority vendor programs are only as effective as the person managing the program at any given time. While corporations spend millions developing and maintaining minority vendor programs, many of those programs provide little in the way of opportunity for minority businesses. This is a prime example of activity intended to give the appearance of progress. That is why so many corporations absolutely refuse to make public the amount of business they are doing with minority businesses, *particularly in comparison to the dollars they spend with competitor businesses*. Even when minority programs have the fervent support of the CEO, they routinely generate little in the way of opportunities for African-American businesses. When questioned, corporations often respond: *We cannot find capable minority suppliers* or *we cannot find African-American suppliers that are large enough to meet our global needs*. As a result, corporations generally require African-American suppliers to function as subcontractors to competitors that provide goods and services directly to major corporations. The resulting dependency stifles competition and relegates African-American firms to a subcontracting role.

IF YOU'VE GOT MY DOLLAR, I DON'T

PREVENTING EXTRACTION

Private-sector Contracting

Corporations will undoubtedly persist in this pattern until African Americans adopt a "no choice" approach to economic inclusion. African Americans should refuse to do business with corporations that do not enter into significant growth-type contracts with African-American suppliers in every area of their business, including professional services. Corporations that demonstrate an immediate willingness to improve *substantially* the **amount** and **quality of business** they do with African-American businesses deserve strong patronage from African Americans.

There are numerous entities that provide information a company needs to implement a minority business development program. They include the National Minority Supplier Development Council (NMSDC) and local organizations that are committed to minority business development.

This variation of an article written for the St. Louis Minority Business Council (SLMBC) reveals how corporations can accelerate and strengthen minority-vendor procurement:

Where Are the Dollars?
A Strategic Approach to MBE Procurement
Remember those TV commercials with the spunky senior who insistently inquired, "Where's the beef?" Similarly, minority businesses nationwide are wondering, *Where are the dollars?* It is a question that emerges as Minority Business Enterprise (MBE) coordinators search relentlessly within their corporate empires for MBE opportunities. At

PREVENTING EXTRACTION

Private-sector Contracting

the same time, top-tier executives enthusiastically proclaim their intent to make increased MBE procurements a strategic goal and a corporate reality.

Why, with all the spirited commitment and expense devoted to marketing corporate MBE programs at trade fairs and related events, and throughout councils nationwide, is MBE procurement floundering?

The answer is simple: MBE procurement is not managed internally as a strategic goal. While effective MBE procurement demands the fervent support of the CEO and a corporate-wide commitment from purchasing managers, *the most important element in successful MBE procurement is a plan.*

Corporations develop annual budgets acknowledging their intent to spend millions procuring goods and services the organization needs to deliver products and services to consumers and other businesses. The reality is that corporations have opportunities—and lots of them—since it is estimated that most large corporations spend a significant portion of their annual operating budget on procurement. Because corporations decide during the annual budgeting process what and how much they are going to purchase, this is a perfect time to develop MBE purchasing budgets. Here is how a corporation can include MBE procurement as part of its annual budgeting process.

■ **Hold a qualification forum, allowing MBEs to come and present their wares.** Identify firms you believe have the core competencies to meet your business needs. While a firm may not have everything you want, make sure the firm delivers excellent quality and service—and that it has a business philosophy compatible with yours. As the MBE firm grows, the other elements you desire will follow.

PREVENTING EXTRACTION

Private-sector Contracting

- **Select several MBE firms that can fulfill needs in diverse areas of your business**, including advertising, accounting, and other professional-service areas where MBE firms are traditionally underutilized.

- **Commit to procuring a substantial amount from each MBE firm.** Secure approval from the CEO and relevant department heads.

- **Work with departments to devise a concrete scope of work for each MBE firm**, thus ensuring targets are met. While this approach may mean diverting business that is currently being performed by another firm to an MBE, such actions are necessary to accomplish a strategic corporate initiative.

- **Repeat the process annually**, continually increasing the amount of business you do with minority vendors.

- **Install internal controls to cultivate relationships with the corporation's African-American suppliers.** African-American businesses often encounter resistance from hostile personnel within organizations. These employees disrupt productive business relationships and often account for the release of qualified minority suppliers.

  As such, organizations must implement a structure that combats these hostile efforts. The structure should give African-American businesses direct access to a senior-level management team that intervenes when an African-American business encounters serious problems or is threatened with contract termination. Before a contract is removed, the team should review the relevant circumstances and meet jointly with the minority supplier and the internal person encouraging termination to determine if the action is warranted.

PREVENTING EXTRACTION

Private-sector Contracting

- **Report.** Most businesses balk at the mention of publishing numbers reflecting the amount of business they are doing with minority businesses. Most are ashamed of their numbers, knowing they are insignificant when compared to the amounts they are spending with nonminority firms. Corporations that want patronage from the African-American community must agree to publish on the Internet audited statistics outlining the amount of total business they do with African-American firms, *by department.*

- **Report when relationships are severed.** When there is a need to sever a relationship with a minority business, the reasons for severing the relationship should be reported to the African-American organization designated to collect such data.

- **Publish biannual report cards.** Without surveillance, corporations will soon lapse into their old practices of barely using African-American firms. The appointed African-American organization must analyze data and identify corporations that are "African-American friendly." Equipped with this information, African Americans can make informed decisions about who is worthy of African-American patronage and who is not.

It really isn't difficult to meet corporate MBE goals. As the advertiser says, "Just do it."

IF YOU'VE GOT MY DOLLAR, I DON'T

PREVENTING EXTRACTION

Federal Government Contracting

The federal government is the largest purchaser of goods and services in the world, procuring more than $200 billion annually. Local and state governments also have significant procurement budgets.

Since African-American tax dollars help finance government contracts, African Americans are justified in insisting that a substantial share of those contracting dollars make their way to African-American firms. There are several ways to accomplish this goal: by reinstating set-aside programs; by ensuring that federal and local procurement processes are well documented and followed to the letter; and by instituting effective forums for redress when African-American firms are dealt with unfairly. Just as participants in the Boston Tea Party were justified in declaring, "No taxation without representation," African Americans are justified in claiming, "No taxation without contract awards."

The following article emphasizes how far competitors will go to prevent African Americans from securing and retaining contracts generally reserved for competitors. Representing extraction at its worst, the events involve the Internal Revenue Service (IRS), the tax collection agency of the U.S. Department of Treasury.

PREVENTING EXTRACTION

Federal Government Contracting

While IRS is one of the most feared organizations in the world, it is not a nameless or faceless organization. Like all entities, it is run by people. At the time of the events outlined in the following article, the head of IRS, Commissioner Charles O. Rossotti, had delegated the agency's procurement responsibilities to two top-level executives, Gregory Rothwell and James Williams. All are aware of events detailed here, which pertain to The Writing Company, the author's firm.

IRS and Treasury Executives Make Their Position Clear: Mega Contract Too Good for African-American Firm

Some may call the award of a mega contract to The Writing Company— a minority-owned business based in St. Louis, Missouri—a major fluke. The Writing Company, however, labels it a miracle, since contracts of such magnitude seldom make their way to minority-owned firms. Looking back, securing the Notice Redesign contract was the easy part, given the events that unfolded—culminating in contract termination and persistent efforts by IRS and Treasury to put The Writing Company out of business.

The saga began in 1997, when IRS contacted The Writing Company about its need for taxpayer Notice Redesign services. Taxpayer notices are those often-dreaded documents notifying millions of taxpayers of taxes, penalties, and interest they owe (or, more happily, tax refunds due them). Challenged with meeting a congressional deadline to improve taxpayer notices, IRS sought to avoid a protracted procurement process by securing services through the 8(a) minority- and women-owned business program, which allows for expedient procurement. Even with a critical deadline looming, not just any vendor would do for Notice Redesign, a highly complex, high-profile contract.

IF YOU'VE GOT MY DOLLAR, I DON'T

PREVENTING EXTRACTION

Federal Government Contracting

While The Writing Company's references attested to the firm's stellar past performance, senior-level IRS executive John Dalrymple needed more. So he asked The Writing Company to rewrite two of IRS's most complex notices in a week, without assistance from IRS. Within days, IRS had the redesigned notices in hand, sharing them throughout the organization and with external parties that had a vested interest in the project's success. The verdict was in. Dalrymple approved the contract award and complimented The Writing Company on a job well done.

Not everyone at IRS and Treasury shared Dalrymple's enthusiasm about the contract award. Nevertheless, the procurement proceeded. Within weeks after The Writing Company delivered its first batch of draft notices, an IRS executive and several other IRS representatives flew to St. Louis to advise The Writing Company's president that two Treasury executives intended to provide The Writing Company's draft notices to Treasury's vendor of choice. National Performance Review (NPR), then under the auspices of Vice President Gore, also secured versions of The Writing Company's draft notices. Before long, Treasury was competing nationwide The Writing Company's versions of taxpayer notices against those produced by Treasury's vendor and by NPR.

The results? Taxpayers expressed resounding approval for The Writing Company's notices. The favorable response did not, however, squelch IRS's and Treasury's efforts to oust The Writing Company.

Eliminating The Writing Company posed its own set of challenges, since the firm produced the best taxpayer notices in IRS's history and continued to meet deadlines despite obstacles and fierce resistance. In an attempt to discover within The Writing Company a reason for contract termination, IRS flew seven representatives to St. Louis to

PREVENTING EXTRACTION

Federal Government Contracting

inspect The Writing Company's site. Upon arrival, the head representative told The Writing Company's president and CEO, Jerroll Sanders, to call employees into the conference room so she could explain to Sanders and her staff the purpose of IRS's visit. Sanders, considering the request highly unorthodox, told the head representative to instead explain to her the purpose of the visit.

After explaining that the team would return the next day to begin the inspection, the representative heading the inspection said her group would need complete access to the facility, as well as the opportunity to interview Sanders' employees without Sanders present. Suspicious of IRS's motives, Sanders engaged her attorney, who barred the IRS team from The Writing Company's site until IRS could explain, in writing, the purpose and scope of the visit. Days later, IRS, The Writing Company's representatives, and local Small Business Administration (SBA) representatives met to discuss the scope of inspection, which IRS provided in writing. They were joined via teleconference by an IRS procurement manager who said a major reason for the visit was to determine the firm's ability to handle follow-on work, since IRS had thousands of notices to revise.

The Writing Company considered the manager's explanation extremely suspect, given the firm's performance, but allowed the inspection nonetheless. Three weeks after the inspection, the IRS procurement manager told Sanders to come to Washington, adding she should bring her attorney. When they met, the manager advised Sanders in surprise fashion that IRS was terminating the contract for "convenience of the government."

PREVENTING EXTRACTION

Federal Government Contracting

The St. Louis SBA representative who participated in the termination meeting via teleconference sent IRS a letter, signed by his superior, criticizing the manner in which IRS conducted the termination. He stated that IRS violated *Federal Acquisition Regulation* (FAR) when it failed to advise SBA of its intent prior to contract termination. The letter also requested that IRS award the new Notice Redesign contract to The Writing Company, since the firm had, by IRS's own admission, performed without deficiency.

Determined to secure a more conclusive explanation for the termination, Sanders, with the help of SBA, arranged to meet with IRS. During the meeting, IRS provided several reasons for contract termination, most notably that it did not want so much knowledge vested in one vendor—knowledge Sanders contends The Writing Company brought to the table.

After concluding the meeting, Sanders contacted her congressional representative to request an inquiry. In response to the congressional inquiry, IRS invited Sanders to Washington, explaining that it intended to reinstate the firm's contract. Once in Washington, Sanders learned of IRS's intent to reinstate only a *small portion* of the lucrative Notice Redesign contract. When asked why it reduced the scope of work, IRS said it needed to slow the project pace because The Writing Company was progressing too rapidly. Sanders presented a counteroffer, asking IRS to extend the contract term rather than reduce the scope of work. IRS refused and ceased reinstatement efforts.

Soon after, IRS removed the Notice Redesign requirement from the minority set-aside program and proceeded to reprocure notice redesign

PREVENTING EXTRACTION

Federal Government Contracting

services—at the $5 million size standard. The reprocurement is undoubtedly the first of many Notice Redesign contracts to follow, totaling an estimated $100 million.

IRS continues to employ heavy-handed tactics designed to put Sanders in her place and The Writing Company out of business. Tactics include denying thousands of dollars in settlement costs the firm is due, withholding invoice payments for over a year, and engineering illegal auditing practices solely to starve the firm financially.

Most recently, IRS attempted to bring a grand jury indictment against Sanders, alleging she had engaged in wage fraud. During a secret, yearlong investigation, federal agents interviewed The Writing Company's former employees, examined Sanders' bank accounts and personal records, and otherwise investigated the firm. Sanders learned of the investigation when two federal agents from Washington appeared unannounced at her site, subpoenaing her to appear before a grand jury. Shocked by the allegations, Sanders presented to agents records and documentation that refuted all charges. By 10 A.M. the following morning, a federal attorney dismissed the investigation based upon the federal agents' findings.

IRS, upon learning the federal wage fraud investigation was dropped, initiated yet another investigation—this time with the U.S. Department of Labor, alleging that The Writing Company had violated the Contract Service Act. If the firm was found guilty, IRS could divert substantial funds it owed The Writing Company to the firm's former employees.

Despite two audits, one site inspection, one federal investigation, and a Department of Labor investigation, Sanders persists in efforts to secure contract reinstatement and the funds IRS owes her firm.

IF YOU'VE GOT MY DOLLAR, I DON'T

PREVENTING EXTRACTION

Federal Government Contracting

African Americans must spearhead an effort to correct federal procurement deficiencies and flagrant abuses, such as those detailed in the preceding article. It is recommended that this effort, undertaken with government funding, should at minimum include the following:

■ **Select a group of procurement specialists to study the federal procurement system. Discern why African Americans are not receiving a representative share of government procurements.** This team must also assess the effectiveness of various federal procurement programs as they relate to African-American vendors, including the 8(a) program, HUBzone program, Small and Disadvantaged Business Utilization program, procurement schedules, and other programs used to procure goods and services. This assessment should include evaluating:

▸ The amount of total federal dollars spent procuring goods and services.

▸ The amount spent with minorities, by racial group.

▸ The number of contracts terminated, by racial group. This information should include the federal agency's explanation as to why it terminated the contract, as well as the African-American business's account of why the contract was terminated.

PREVENTING EXTRACTION

Federal Government Contracting

- **Recommend changes that ensure the federal procurement process is fair.** Based upon the assessment, African Americans should advocate that Congress legislate changes needed to enable African-American businesses to participate more fully in the federal procurement system.

- **Determine if existing forums enable African-American contractors to effectively redress discriminatory contracting actions.** The Writing Company's experience with IRS, and the experiences of other 8(a) vendors, indicates that African-American firms are not served by current Boards of Contract Appeals, which at present adjudicate contract claims and disputes. While the U.S. Department of Justice holds large companies such as HBE and Denny's accountable for racial discrimination, similar acts committed by federal agencies go unaddressed. The Justice Department should have a separate department charged solely with reviewing and resolving claims of racial discrimination in federal contracting.

- **Require ongoing reporting of contracting data by racial group.** Government agencies should report contract information by racial group, including awards, terminations, and so forth.

PREVENTING EXTRACTION

State and Local Contracting

With regard to *state* and *local* government contracting, African Americans can take the actions that follow:

- **Form an African-American vendor association that is headed by a Board of Directors consisting of African-American business owners.** Include surveillance as a key responsibility of the African-American vendor association. The organization should serve as an advocate for grievances related to African-American contractors and should evaluate newly introduced procurement legislation to determine its effect on the African-American community. It is unlikely that any organization can represent African-American businesses as vigorously as African-American business owners themselves.

- **Acquire data about state and local entities' procurements.** Determine how much business the state or local entity is doing, by department, with African-American firms.

- **Develop a procurement plan.** Working with local governments, develop a procurement plan to ensure African Americans receive a significant share of contracting dollars awarded. Create a steering committee to work with contracting officials to implement the plan and track progress.

- **Ensure the procurement plan includes minority set-aside contracts for African-American businesses.** Without set-aside programs, minority firms seem only to survive. With set-aside programs, minority firms thrive. Courts, however, are making it increasingly difficult for governments to justify the existence of set-aside and other minority vendor programs:

PREVENTING EXTRACTION

State and Local Contracting

▸ *Richmond v. Croson* represents the Supreme Court's initial attack on minority vendor contracting programs. In *Croson*, the Court ruled that states with minority vendor or set-aside programs must demonstrate that strong reasons exist for having such a program. The court also ruled that the program must be narrowly tailored to correct specific wrongs. As such, states must not only identify the discrimination, past or present, but also ensure that the remedy is crafted to offset the specific discrimination identified.

▸ *Adarand Constructors v. Peña* applied a similar standard, this time to federal minority vendor and set-aside programs. *Adarand* requires that the federal government establish a "factual predicate," meaning that the government must prove through either a study or other valid means that past or present racial discrimination has adversely affected minority contractors, thereby necessitating a specific remedy.

In response, states and the federal government have embarked upon studies to document how discrimination has affected minority firms' ability to grow and prosper. Such data are often presented in the form of a disparity study. Even when data confirm a disparity exists between the *number of minority vendors available to perform contracts* and the *percentage of contracting dollars those vendors receive*, the courts continue their hostile attack on race-based programs:

PREVENTING EXTRACTION

State and Local Contracting

▶ In *Engineering Contractors v. Dade County*, the Court questioned the underlying assumptions of the program, requiring Dade County to demonstrate that the disparity was in fact **caused by racial discrimination and was not attributable to other factors**, such as the personal capabilities of business owners.

▶ In *Webster v. Fulton*, the Court questioned the **validity of census data** used in the disparity study.

▶ In *AGC of Ohio v. Drabik*, the Court challenged the **length of the program**, thereby requiring states and municipalities to reaffirm the need for set-aside programs with increased frequency.

Why do the courts persist in requiring government entities to prove what everyone else knows? Are judges not well versed in American history, which includes over two hundred years of institutionalized slavery (much of it Supreme Court-ordained) and almost 70 years of racial discrimination under the Supreme Court-introduced "separate but equal" doctrine? Are the courts not aware of Jim Crow laws and their contributions to Black disadvantagedness? And why are legislators embracing the courts' actions, urging an "amend it, don't end it" approach to affirmative action and set-aside programs? Because set-aside programs are effective. They divert significant dollars—long enjoyed by competitors—to African Americans.

PREVENTING EXTRACTION

State and Local Contracting

Hence, African Americans must join nationwide to thwart the Court's efforts to make set-aside and other minority vendor programs a phenomenon of the past. Locally, African Americans must insist that states reinstate set-aside programs when data warrant. While the courts have not abolished set-aside programs altogether, they are definitely making it increasingly difficult for state and local governments to introduce and maintain set-aside programs.

PREVENTING EXTRACTION

Legal System

The American legal system is inappropriately named the system of justice. The integrity of the legal system rests with judges and their "good faith" pledge to be fair and equitable when administering the law. Like other major systems in the American fabric, the justice system is distorted by hostile competitors who use the rules of law to obstruct African Americans who seek financial remedies through the legal process. The American legal system is merely a chess game where those with money and political clout control the board and shift the game pieces at will. The legal system extracts millions of dollars from African Americans by rendering unfair judgments, dismissing cases without justification, and taking other hostile legal actions.

The legal system: adversary of African Americans. From the very beginning, the legal system has failed to serve the interests of African Americans. The following are a series of events that characterize the court's long-standing hostility toward the African-American community.

The events begin with the *Dred Scott* case (*Dred Scott v. Sandford*). Scott had lived with his master in free territory for seven years. Upon returning to Missouri, a slave state, Scott sued for his freedom and that of his family. The Supreme Court's 1857 *Dred Scott* decision addresses a number of legal questions that prevailed at that time, including whether slaves were citizens of the United States and thus entitled to constitutional guarantees enjoyed by Whites.

PREVENTING EXTRACTION

Legal System

According to the Supreme Court, neither the *Declaration of Independence* nor the *Constitution* meant to assign rights to slaves or their descendants, even those who were free. In the Court's opinion, persons of African origin were beings of an "inferior order." Chief Justice Roger Brooke Taney, who wrote the Supreme Court decision, stated: ". . . the public history of every European nation displays it [the inferiority of persons of African descent] in a manner too plain to be mistaken." He continued:

> They [African Americans] had for more than a century before been regarded as beings of an inferior order, and altogether unfit to associate with the white race either in social or political relations, and so far inferior that they had no rights which the white man was bound to respect, and that the negro might justly and lawfully be reduced to slavery for his benefit. He was bought and sold, and treated as an ordinary article of merchandise and traffic whenever a profit could be made by it. This opinion was at that time fixed and universal in the civilized portion of the white race. It was regarded as an axiom in morals as well as in politics which no one thought of disputing or supposed to be open to dispute, and men in every grade and position in society daily and habitually acted upon it in their private pursuits, as well as in matters of public concern, without doubting for a moment the correctness of this opinion.

Thus, according to the Supreme Court, Blacks were so inferior to Whites they could not be considered people.

It took a presidential proclamation to free the slaves. President Abraham Lincoln, who disagreed with the *Dred Scott* ruling, used the Second Confiscation Act (July 17, 1862) to

PREVENTING EXTRACTION

Legal System

emancipate slaves in Confederate states. The act allowed the president to confiscate *property* from those rebelling against the Union—namely the Confederacy. Since citizens in the Confederate states regarded slaves as property, Lincoln used his confiscation authority to declare slaves in those states free.

The Emancipation Proclamation of 1863, which freed slaves in Confederate states, preceded a number of Constitutional amendments and congressional acts that recognized further the rights of African Americans, including:

- **The 13th Amendment**, enacted in 1865 to free slaves who had not been freed by the Emancipation Proclamation.

- **The 14th Amendment** (ratified in 1868), which corrected the *Dred Scott* decision. The act states: "All persons born or naturalized in the United States . . . are citizens of the United States." It also afforded African Americans due process and equal protection under the law.

- **The 15th Amendment** (ratified in 1870), which established African Americans' right to vote.

- **The Civil Rights Act of 1866**, which declared that all persons born in the United States are citizens with full rights under the Constitution.

- **The Civil Rights Act of 1875**, which granted all citizens the same rights, including the right to use public accommodations; serve on juries; make contracts; testify in court; purchase, hold, and dispose of property; and fully enjoy equal benefit of all laws.

PREVENTING EXTRACTION

Legal System

> On October 16, 1883, the Supreme Court again demonstrated its hostility toward Black America. The Court declared the 1875 Civil Rights Act unconstitutional, stating that while Blacks might be people, they were not people in the context referenced in the Constitution.
>
> The court continued its hostile position against Black America in *Plessy v. Ferguson* (1896). The court ruled that an African American named Plessy, who brought suit, did not have the right to ride in the White passenger section of a railway train. Hence, the court ordained the doctrine of "separate but equal," further institutionalizing White privilege and Black disadvantagedness.
>
> **It took 165 years for the United States Supreme Court to begin to recognize the full rights of African Americans.** The Supreme Court of the United States was created by the Judiciary Act of September 24, 1789. It took until May 17, 1954, in *Brown v. Board of Education of Topeka*, for the Court to recognize the citizenship and rights of African Americans—but only in the area of public education. The ruling in *Brown* reversed the *Plessy* ruling by stating that "the doctrine of 'separate but equal' has no place." It took another 10 years and legislative passage of the Civil Rights Act of 1964—the most sweeping civil-rights legislation ever—to end segregated public facilities and accommodations, which the Court's *Plessy* ruling sanctioned.

IF YOU'VE GOT MY DOLLAR, I DON'T

PREVENTING EXTRACTION

Legal System

Court resumes its adversarial role with Black America. Today, the Supreme Court has resumed its hostile relationship with Black America, rendering a series of decisions that attack and erode affirmative action programs and other gains African Americans have realized. As such, African Americans must seek to achieve through legislation what the Supreme Court and its lower courts deny. When the courts overturn laws and legal decisions that provide redress to African Americans, we must refashion our legal positions and arguments, continuously looking for ways to eliminate the disparities we know affect our daily lives. After all, history demonstrates that if African Americans had relied upon the courts for justice, we may well have entered the new millennium shackled by the bonds of slavery.

While some progress has been made, the courts still fail to protect the interests of African Americans, as revealed by the following two articles: "Judge Not Sorry for Racist Notes" and "Small Business Owners Beware: Hanging Up Your Shingle Could Be Bad for Business."

PREVENTING EXTRACTION

Legal System

Judge Not Sorry for Racist Notes
Reprinted from AltaVista: LIVE! (Internet) 01/30/00 19:10 EST

SPOKANE, Wash. (AP)—A federal judge says he doesn't have to apologize for notes he exchanged with courtroom staff that contained racially offensive language and off-color remarks about ethnic groups.

The Spokesman-Review reported Sunday that U.S. District Judge Alan McDonald wrote "Ah is im po tent!" in one note while a black man was testifying.

In a note court clerk Pam Posada gave the judge, she wrote: "It smells like oil in here—too many 'Greasers.'" The courtroom was full of Hispanic defendants and lawyers at the time.

McDonald said the notes were never intended for the public and were being misinterpreted.

"I don't need to apologize for them because they were never intended to be in a situation where they could be misunderstood," McDonald told The Spokesman-Review.

Most of the notes were provided to the newspaper by Kathryn Blankenship, who sued over being fired in 1995 after spending nine years as McDonald's court reporter in Yakima. A federal appeals court dismissed her 1997 lawsuit; she has appealed.

McDonald said Blankenship had performance problems and a vendetta against him.

Other notes written by McDonald and Posada were given to the newspaper by Spokane attorney William Powell, who had saved notes that he and another attorney fished out of a wastebasket during a 1990 trial.

IF YOU'VE GOT MY DOLLAR, I DON'T

PREVENTING EXTRACTION

Legal System

William Fremming Nielsen, chief judge for the federal district in eastern Washington that includes Yakima, asked McDonald to explain the notes to The Spokesman-Review and sat in on the interview.

He said he was satisfied with McDonald's explanations.

"Any communication that's short is subject to misinterpretation," Nielsen said.

McDonald, 72, was nominated for the lifetime judgeship by President Reagan and confirmed by the Senate in 1985. He has been on senior status since December 1996, drawing his full $141,300 salary while handling a reduced caseload.

Making disparaging comments about people in court violates rules for federal judges, said Stephen Gillers, a legal ethics expert at New York University School of Law.

"Speaking generally, if the notes reflect religious or racial animosity or demeaning comments, that's a violation of the code of professional conduct for U.S. judges. There could be a sanction, including a public reprimand," Gillers said.

Blankenship told the newspaper that some of the notes passed between the judge and Posada were also passed to her. One concerned a black plaintiff—Jesse Jackson Jr., no relation to the civil rights leader—in a trial in San Diego where McDonald was a visiting judge.

Jackson Jr. had been vice president of Imperial Savings Association, a California S&L that failed in the 1980s. He sued Imperial in 1991 over his firing, **but McDonald ruled against him in a directed verdict, ending the trial before it went to the jury**. [Author's bold type.]

PREVENTING EXTRACTION

Legal System

In one note, which Blankenship said McDonald passed to her while Jackson was testifying, the judge wrote, "Ah is Im po tent!"

McDonald said the note referred to himself, not Jackson. "This is a term of self-deprecation that I employ," McDonald said.

Another note, which could not be linked to a specific trial, referred to Mormons and other ethnic groups.

"He's been a con man for a long time!" Posada wrote.

The judge replied: "Yes, and in my experience, a Mormon money man makes the Jews and Chinese look like rank amateurs!"

In his interview with the newspaper, McDonald said: "I'm sure that I made the remark out of respect for the Mormons I know."

Posada told The Spokesman-Review she couldn't comment because of rules for courthouse employees. But she added that Blankenship was trying to use the newspaper to "harass the judge and embarrass the system, knowing that those of us who know the truth can't be heard."

Reprinted with permission of The Associated Press.

IF YOU'VE GOT MY DOLLAR, I DON'T

PREVENTING EXTRACTION

Legal System

Small Business Owners Beware:
Hanging Up Your Shingle Could Be Bad for Business

For over a century, the telephone has been the most integral tool in contacting potential and existing customers. More than 150 million phones in this country keep businesses and consumers connected. Simply put, without a telephone, your days of business aren't just numbered— they're over.

That's what Tim Person, Sr., found out when his local phone service provider, Southwestern Bell Telephone, disconnected his number 60 times between September 1982 and March 1983. As a result, he lost his biggest customer and his business nearly collapsed.

Hard-Fought Battles and Trusted Advice

Even before difficulties with Southwestern Bell, Tim Person faced a daunting challenge. After 12 years of testimony, cross-country hearings, and vehement opposition from the major players in the transportation industry, Tim Person's company, Allstates Transworld Van Lines, became the first minority-owned enterprise to win a nationwide operating license.

Person's investment of more than a million dollars in pursuing the license paid off, as the company secured a major contract with the U.S. Department of Defense to ship the household goods of military personnel being transferred across the country.

Still reeling from the victory and struggling to get his now-nationwide business off the ground, Person's company faced a period of financial difficulty almost two years later, in late 1982.

He consulted a lawyer to plan ways of reducing his monthly expenditures for a brief span of time. Among other strategies, the lawyer informed

PREVENTING EXTRACTION

Legal System

Person that he could delay his payment for Yellow Page directory advertising—while still paying his bill for local and long-distance calls—without any disruption in telephone service. In the end, taking that advice turned into a far more insidious dilemma than any temporary financial troubles.

No Dial Tone, No Business
Between September 1982 and March 1983, the local phone company disconnected telephone service to Allstates 60 times in its efforts to collect payment for the company's Yellow Page directory advertising. Unable to communicate with clients, Allstates began losing customers, including its major contract with the Department of Defense. Devastated by the losses, the company filed for bankruptcy in 1984.

For the next few years, Person organized Allstates' financial affairs and pondered how his promising company had reached its current state. If only his telephone service—the lifeline to his customers—had not been cut off, his company would have recovered from its temporary fiscal setback.

Recalling the lawyer's assertion about the phone company's supposed inability to disconnect his service for nonpayment of directory advertising, he began to contact the Public Service Commissions and Utilities Boards in several states. Their letters—from states as varied as Oklahoma and Hawaii—bore striking resemblance:

"A phone customer who does not pay his directory advertising charges will not have his phone service terminated as a result."
—Montana Public Service Commission

"Under Iowa Utilities Board rules, directory advertising is not regulated and a utility cannot disconnect for non-payment of unregulated service."

IF YOU'VE GOT MY DOLLAR, I DON'T

PREVENTING EXTRACTION

Legal System

> *"Local exchange companies in California are not authorized to disconnect telephone service as a result of non-payment of Yellow Pages advertising."*
> —California Public Utilities Commission

> *"Customers cannot be disconnected for nonpayment of Yellow Page advertising. . . ."*
> —Wisconsin Public Service Commission

The Next Battle

These revelations prompted Person to file a complaint with AT&T, his long-distance telephone service provider. He was informed that his complaint stemmed from actions taken by Southwestern Bell Telephone Company, the local exchange provider for AT&T that bore responsibility for Yellow Pages advertising. Faced with Person's complaint, a Southwestern Bell representative reportedly claimed that the company never interrupted Allstates' phone service. She stated instead that it was not Southwestern Bell's practice to disconnect service for nonpayment of directory advertising.

Unsatisfied with the phone company's response—which he knew to be untrue—Person took his fight to the next level: court. In 1995, Allstates filed suit against Southwestern Bell for its repeated disruptions in phone service. The jury apparently agreed that the phone company bore responsibility for nearly wiping out Person's business and awarded Allstates $12 million ($4 million in actual damages and $8 million in punitive damages).

Elated with his vindication, Person got back to the business of building his moving company's customer base. Meanwhile, Southwestern Bell began the process of appealing the jury verdict.

PREVENTING EXTRACTION

Legal System

It's Not Over Until It's Over

Allstates' victory, however, was short-lived. Eighteen months later, a judge overturned the jury award, ruling that in 1982 and 1983, the phone service and Yellow Pages directory advertising were linked, so Southwestern Bell was justified in interrupting service for any sum due. The judge also ruled that Allstates could not secure another chance for a trial.

The judge's decision might not be so troubling if it were not based on ambiguous grounds. There is no consensus about whether Southwestern Bell's telephone service and Yellow Page advertising were legally interconnected in the early 1980s.

An attorney with the Common Carrier Bureau of the Federal Communications Commission (FCC) disputes the judge's conclusion: "It would appear to be unreasonable for the local phone company to disconnect service only for failure to pay Yellow Pages charges."

Today, Person is frustrated to find that multiple government agencies, public utilities commissions, and phone carriers (other than Southwestern Bell) agree with his argument that he is unable to present in court.

Since the hearts of hostile competitors are not changed by the adorning of robes, the legal system demands systemic changes and safeguards to ensure African Americans receive equal treatment:

IF YOU'VE GOT MY DOLLAR, I DON'T

PREVENTING EXTRACTION

Legal System

- **Prevent judges from unilaterally reducing jury awards.** Hostile competitors sitting as judges have the authority to unilaterally reverse judgments, thus removing millions from African Americans. Judges should not have authority to unilaterally reduce jury awards.

- **Collect and publish race-based data on case outcomes.** Judges might be more accountable for equity and fairness if their case outcomes are published, by race of litigant, including case dismissals, unilateral reduction in awards, and other important legal rulings. While some may argue that publication would taint the legal process by compelling judges to render favorably on behalf of a percentage of the African Americans that come before them, African Americans would argue that race is already a factor in the legal decision-making process.

- **Abolish lifetime terms for judges.** Judges that serve on the U.S. Supreme Court, U.S. District Courts, and U.S. Courts of Appeals receive lifetime appointments. They are appointed by the President and confirmed by the United States Senate. While many presume that judges, including Supreme Court justices, are objective, nothing is further from the truth.

  As we all do, judges make decisions in the context of their values, ideological views, partisan perspectives, and racial attitudes. Thus, judges are free to make sweeping policy changes with little accountability, particularly when interpreting law that is undefined or poorly defined. That is why politicians give such serious consideration to the

PREVENTING EXTRACTION

Legal System

ideological and political persuasions of prospective judges during judicial appointments. They recognize that a judge's perspective imprints decision-making: Is the appointee a Democrat or a Republican? Is he or she a liberal, moderate, or conservative? What are the appointee's views on abortion and affirmative action?

Like all human beings, judges (including Supreme Court justices) must be held accountable. Thus, judges should be reconfirmed, after serving a specified term, at hearings that include substantial citizen involvement. As the actions of Judge McDonald and the response from his superior, William Fremming Nielsen, demonstrate, judges must be accountable to those outside their profession. Only then will a true system of checks and balances exist.

- **No taxation without "free" legal representation.** Since data reveal that African Americans are subject to disparate treatment in every walk of life, *the U.S. government owes African Americans an effective, simple, no-cost system for litigating discrimination lawsuits.* African Americans contribute taxes to the national Treasury just as competitors do, yet Congress and other lawmakers do very little to ensure African Americans receive the Constitutional guarantees to which they are entitled. Is it reasonable to expect African Americans to spend their own dollars suing for Constitutional rights others automatically enjoy? Absolutely not! Whatever it takes, whatever it costs, Congress, the president, and local, regional, and state lawmaking bodies have a Constitutional responsibility to ensure African Americans are allowed to compete on equal

PREVENTING EXTRACTION

Legal System

footing. Competitors argue that a "no-cost" litigation system will cause a flood of discrimination lawsuits. They are probably right, since at every turn, African Americans are subject to discriminatory acts that deny them financial opportunities. African Americans who initiated discrimination litigation anytime within the last 20 years and had their action dismissed or reduced by more than 10 percent should have an automatic right to appeal via the no-cost system, irrespective of any statutes of limitations.

■ **Uniform application of case law.** Laws are currently established by the *U.S. Constitution*, the *legislative process*, and *case law*. Case law is a collection of nationwide court decisions made by judges adjudicating cases and responding to motions and legal pleadings. When arguing a case, attorneys often lend support to their legal position by referring to case law. Since case law usually contains differing opinions on the same matter, hostile judges can justify unfair rulings against African Americans by citing case law or creating precedents.

African Americans must pursue the creation of a legal clearinghouse that establishes a prevailing court opinion on legal matters that judges are bound to follow unless they are establishing a precedent. Precedents must be reviewed by and approved by a higher level court. If approved, the precedent becomes the prevailing legal opinion that governs judicial decisions. Only then can African Americans be assured that the rules of competition are being applied equally to all.

PREVENTING EXTRACTION

Criminal Justice System

The criminal justice system extracts enormous wealth from African Americans. The system is designed to ensure the prosecution, punishment, and supposed rehabilitation of those who commit crimes. It is a nationwide network that includes police; criminal lawyers; prosecutors; public defenders; criminal courts; and local, state, and federal prisons. At every step of the criminal justice process, improper treatment of African Americans—particularly males—is the rule:

- *Malice Green*, viciously bludgeoned to death in 1992 after a confrontation with Detroit police officers Walter Budzyn and Larry Nevers.

- *Rodney King*, videotaped while being brutally beaten by Los Angeles police officers, all of whom were later acquitted. The acquittal sparked widespread rioting and civil unrest.

- *Amadou Diallo*, killed by 19 of 41 gunshots fired by New York City police officers (who were later acquitted). The fatal shooting of Diallo at his Bronx home further demonstrates the fatal errors police officers nationwide reserve for African Americans.

- *Ellen Reasonover*, released from prison 16 years after a federal judge ruled her trial "fundamentally unfair." The crux of the prosecution's case rested on two jailhouse witnesses who alleged that Reasonover, while jailed, had confessed her involvement in the murder of a St. Louis

PREVENTING EXTRACTION

Criminal Justice System

gas station attendant. Although two secretly taped conversations of Reasonover could have helped her defense, the prosecution—which knew of the tapes—withheld the taped evidence to accomplish Reasonover's conviction.

■ Hundreds of African Americans who were wrongly convicted when Los Angeles police detectives planted and tampered with evidence.

Rampant disparity in the criminal justice system is also engulfing African-American youth and destroying their lives.

The system's crimes against young African Americans. On April 25, 2000, the national organization Building Blocks for Youth released "And Justice for Some," which demonstrates, shockingly and statistically, the extent to which African-American youth are subject to unfair treatment at every stage of the criminal justice process. From arrest to detention to court to incarceration, minority youth—and particularly those who are African-American—are overrepresented at every juncture of the juvenile justice system. Even more distressingly, minority youth are more likely than White youth to be tried in the adult criminal court system—even when the offense is the same. **In 1997, admissions to state prisons involved 7,400 youth under the age of 18—and 58 percent of these youth were African-American.**

PREVENTING EXTRACTION

Criminal Justice System

As report co-authors Eileen Poe Yamagata and Michael Jones summarize, "Processing decisions in many states and local juvenile justice systems are not racially neutral. Minority youth are more likely than White youth to become involved in the system[,] with their disproportionate involvement increasing at each stage of the process." Additionally, the report highlights that:

- African-American youth are more likely than White youth to be formally charged in juvenile court—especially when the offense involves drugs.

- When charged with the same offenses as White youth, African-American youth with no prior admissions are **six times more likely** than their White counterparts to be incarcerated in public facilities for juvenile offenders.

- In the American criminal justice system, an estimated 200,000 youth are tried as adults each year. Whatever the offense, African-American youth are more likely than White youth to have their cases judicially waived to adult court. In criminal cases tried in adult court, youth are more likely to receive adult sanctions such as prison and the death penalty.

- In 1997, White youth received prison sentences in 26 percent of their court cases, whereas African-American youth received prison sentences in 32 percent of their court cases.

IF YOU'VE GOT MY DOLLAR, I DON'T

PREVENTING EXTRACTION

Criminal Justice System

Why are African-American and other minority youth so highly represented in the criminal justice system? Research findings point to racial bias against minority youth within the juvenile justice system. There is also a "cumulative disadvantage" for minority youth: Because racial disparity is most pronounced at the early points of involvement (arrest and detention), overrepresentation tends to accumulate and spiral at later stages of the juvenile system process.

Yamagata and Jones conclude that recent judicial sentiment has veered from the juvenile justice system's original mission to treat and rehabilitate young offenders. Instead, the judicial trend favors punishment and accountability in the name of public safety. As such, minority youth—and particularly African-American youth—receive disparate and harsher treatment within this climate that demands more severe punishment. Our juvenile justice system, Yamagata and Jones believe, is "separate but unequal."

Almost immediately following the report's publication, noted *Washington Post* opinion columnist William Raspberry on April 28, 2000, commented on its findings. In doing so, he conjectured why there are such blatant disparities in dealing with minority youth in the criminal justice system:

PREVENTING EXTRACTION

Criminal Justice System

You could call it rank racism, but that's too easy. It isn't that officials at the various option points between arrest and disposition say the kid is black, so I'll do X, or he's white, so I'll only do Y. The greater likelihood is that they, like the rest of us, respond to the pictures in our heads.

Mention Littleton or Jonesboro, and the picture is likely to be of "troubled" teenagers—perhaps from families that give them too little attention, from schools where they are put down as nerds or geeks, or from other circumstances that "explain" their aberrational behavior.

Mention a shooting in South Central or Hough or Southeast Washington, and the picture is likely to be of an armed thug—bristling for trouble and richly deserving of the full weight of the law.

In the one case, the questions are about what went wrong; in the other, they are about how best to protect ourselves. . . .

Perceptions guide us without our permission. They take control when we are formulating thoughts and opinions and making decisions. How else can one explain a system that allows six times as many African-American youth with no prior offenses to be incarcerated than White youth with the same background?

IF YOU'VE GOT MY DOLLAR, I DON'T

PREVENTING EXTRACTION

Criminal Justice System

That is why we so desperately require a criminal justice system with stringent safeguards. Injustices and the resulting criminal proceedings remove enormous wealth and vitality from the African-American community, while funneling billions to competitors in the form of salaries, prison construction contracts, prison supplies, service contracts, and legal fees. America continues to build even more correctional facilities in anticipation of more African-American prisoners to come.

PREVENTING EXTRACTION

Criminal Justice System

Judges. Judges are free to "reign" without accountability. African Americans must be able to ensure that judges administer the law with fairness and integrity. The following initiatives are therefore sorely needed:

- **Career information on cases heard, by judge.** Data should provide synopsis of the type of case, category of crime, the race of the defendant and the victim, sentence, and other relevant information. Some may argue that this requirement will place undue pressure on judges to sentence according to statistics. Given current criminal justice statistics, African Americans have every right to have before them data they can evaluate to determine if judges are carrying out their duties fairly and equitably.

- **Parole information.** Publish parole application information, including the crime committed, time served, race of the plaintiff, names of persons on the parole board, decision of the parole board, and comments from the parole applicant.

Standard penalties. Parameters for penalties are defined by legislators and lawmaking bodies. African Americans must take immediate action when lawmaking bodies assign disparate penalties for similar crimes. For example, the United States Sentencing Commission, created by Congress, assigned a harsher penalty for crack possession than for cocaine possession. Crack is the drug of choice for many African-American drug users and cocaine is the drug of choice for many White drug users. Both drugs are derivatives of cocaine and are very similar. The harsher penalty for crack helps account for

PREVENTING EXTRACTION

Criminal Justice System

the disproportionate number of African Americans now imprisoned. While the media reveals that many high-profile political leaders have used cocaine, countless African-American males spend their prime years in prison for essentially the same offense. Although the African-American community has complained of disparate penalties for years, neither Congress nor the Sentencing Commission has offered a remedy. The community's call for fairness has been and will continue to be ignored until African Americans engage in *sustained, grassroots advocacy to accomplish needed change.*

Public prosecutors. These legal practitioners are vigorous in their prosecution efforts, particularly when crimes or events are high-profile. These officials have been known to withhold or falsify evidence to obtain convictions. Congress must enact legislation that specifies a predefined sentence for prosecutors who withhold or falsify evidence. When evidence is withheld or altered, the convicted party should automatically receive a new trial.

Criminal lawyers. Attorneys of all races prey on African Americans and other disadvantaged citizens who simply do not have the information they need to make informed decisions about which attorneys to select. This lack of legal resources is critical, given that about 66 percent of the male prison population is African-American. This statistic implies much, including that African Americans are not receiving adequate legal representation. Countless attorneys have exhausted the finances of African-American litigants and defendants and then

PREVENTING EXTRACTION

Criminal Justice System

either failed to deliver or dropped the case altogether. African Americans must work to require attorneys to report the following, absent the name of the litigant:

- Brief description of the case.

- Case outcome.

- Race of defendant.

- Race of plaintiff.

- Manner in which the defense was funded (was it paid with personal funds or was it state-funded).

- Amount charged litigant.

Public defenders. Many African Americans are forced to place their entire future in the hands of public defenders who, other than amassing a record of "wins," have little incentive to vigorously defend their clients. Also, many public defenders do not have the resources to mount the type of defense a particular case might warrant. As such, many African Americans are imprisoned not because the facts prove them guilty beyond a reasonable doubt, but because they simply lack the resources to present a credible defense. America should abandon the current public defender system and instead issue vouchers that defendants can use to compensate attorneys of their choice. A voucher process and a requirement that attorneys publish their case results on the Internet will enable African Americans to make sound choices when it comes to entrusting defense attorneys with their lives.

PREVENTING EXTRACTION

Criminal Justice System

Plea bargaining. Too often, African-American males who are erroneously arrested and charged must choose between pleading guilty to a lesser crime or standing trial for a much more serious crime with significantly harsher penalties. As a result, many African Americans are managing risk by pleading guilty to crimes they did not commit. Since African Americans are often the subject of evidence-planting and other acts that lead to prosecution and conviction, plea bargaining should involve a "mini-jury" process. A jury team should interview the alleged perpetrator and the prosecution's evidence to determine if the plea bargain is too harsh, given the allegations, evidence, and related circumstances.

The police. The police are African Americans' worst nightmare, since they are largely at war with the African-American community. Wrongful arrests, unjustified ticketing, and evidence-planting entangle countless African Americans in the criminal justice system, extracting enormous wealth. In every town and municipality, the police are supposed to protect and serve. As such, African Americans must focus on stopping police mistreatment of African Americans. Clearly, a new, more effective system of law enforcement is needed nationwide.

■ **Citizen Police Review Boards.** These boards should become a federally mandated component of every police structure. They must have both investigative and enforcement

PREVENTING EXTRACTION

Criminal Justice System

powers, as well as the authority to oversee complaints against police. Additionally, this board would have authority to overturn the findings of police department Internal Affairs departments when warranted, to bring charges against police officers on behalf of the people, and to order dismissal of police officers. The boards would operate with complete autonomy from the police department and consist of both community representatives and representatives from other communities.

- ■ **Reporting.** African Americans can help enact legislation that requires every police department in the country to publish a report card on the Internet. The report should detail statistics on police activities. Report data would allow African Americans and others to identify police jurisdictions that are hostile to African Americans. For example, while in court in the city of Charlack, Missouri, to resolve a traffic violation, I noticed that about 98 percent of the defendants were African-American. The community, however, is predominantly White. As I awaited my appearance before the judge, I also noted that African Americans received significantly harsher penalties and much larger fines than non-African Americans. In addition to constituting blatant discrimination, these excessive fines represent a significant outflow of cash, contributed primarily by African Americans. If Charlack were required to publish fine and arrest statistics by race, it might adopt a

PREVENTING EXTRACTION

Criminal Justice System

more equitable approach to administering the law. African Americans would have immediate access to data that would justify, if need be, African Americans suing the city's police force for racial discrimination. Data available for public review on the Internet and at the library should include:

▶ Demographics of the municipality's population.

▶ Statistics by race and sex on police stops, tickets issued, fines assessed, and other similar information.

▶ Arrest information by race, crime, and prior arrests or convictions (if any), along with a brief synopsis of charges.

▶ Variable Internet database search capability, so citizens can review arrest rates by crime, race, and even officer.

PREVENTING EXTRACTION

Lending and Insurance

The areas of lending and insurance perpetuate marked economic disparities between African Americans and their competitors.

Loans

It is widely recognized that African Americans have significant difficulty securing loans. African Americans must insist that the federal government require lending institutions to reveal loan data on applicants by race (but without revealing the applicants' names). Data provided should include:

- **Total number of loans made and total number of loans declined.**

- **Applicant profiles (race, income, sex, credit rating).** While loan applications currently do not ask for race, the prospective borrower meets with the loan officer, who is critically involved in the loan process. Therefore the race of the loan applicant is usually apparent. The inclusion of race on loan applications will help, not injure, African Americans.

- **Loan processing time.**

- **Reasons for denial or acceptance.**

- **Type of loan (business or personal loan).**

- **Census tract of the applicant.**

Insurance

For African Americans, the process for determining insurance premiums remains grossly unfair. For that reason, African Americans should advocate the following:

PREVENTING EXTRACTION

Lending and Insurance

- **One rate for the state.** The current system of insurance penalizes persons for where they live. Many African Americans—who bear no responsibility for the crime that occurs in their neighborhood—pay higher insurance premiums because they live in disadvantaged areas. As such, African Americans should advocate that insurance companies use a statewide rate for each category of insurance, particularly homeowner's, renter's, and automobile insurance.

- **Race-neutral damage awards.** When determining damages for wrongful death or for injury, attorneys and insurers consider a host of factors, including foregone earnings. Because Whites generally have higher wages than African Americans—largely attributable to generations of White privilege—Whites often receive higher damage or wrongful death awards. Hence, Whites are valued more highly than African Americans both in life and in death. To narrow the wealth divide, African Americans must insist on a process that treats Whites and African Americans equally with regard to liability and wrongful death settlements.

The insurance industry is characterized by discriminatory practices that are far more insidious and prevalent than any American would care to admit. The following article appeared in the November 7, 2000, edition of the *St. Louis Post-Dispatch*, alleging discriminatory practices:

PREVENTING EXTRACTION

Lending and Insurance

Reliable is accused of discrimination in lawsuit

Reliable Life Insurance Co.'s agents were told not to sell standard life insurance policies to African Americans, and sold them overpriced "burial" policies instead, according to a class action lawsuit pending against the company.

The suit, filed on behalf of two policyholders, accuses Reliable of "race discrimination, fraud, deception, cheat, artifice, trickery, trick, coercion, extortion and/or oppression."

A company spokesman said Reliable does not comment on pending lawsuits.

The suit was filed last month, shortly before Reliable's parent company appointed an African American as Reliable's president. Unitrin Inc. of Chicago on Oct. 27 named Don M. Royster to head Webster Groves-based Reliable.

Reliable specializes in selling life insurance policies for relatively small amounts, usually to low-income people.

The policies are often sold as a way to cover the cost of a burial.

The suit, filed by lawyer Diane Nygaard of Leawood, Kan., charges that Reliable told its agents not to offer better insurance policies to black clients. Reliable charged higher premiums to blacks than whites, the suit alleges.

The suit said Reliable overcharged for its policies—often collecting more in premiums than it would pay if a client died.

For instance, she said a corporate predecessor of Reliable sold Phoebe Watkins a $250 life insurance policy in 1943. Watkins, of Lawrence,

PREVENTING EXTRACTION

Lending and Insurance

Kan., faithfully paid 14 cents a week for 57 years. Watkins has now paid $415 for a policy that would pay only $250 if she died.

Radford Moore, of Kansas City, bought two policies totaling $6,000 in 1982. He paid $19.44 per month until he turned 65 last year. After turning 65, Moore was no longer required to pay premiums, but the amount of insurance dropped to $2,000.

Moore has now paid nearly $4,000 in premiums on a policy that will pay $2,000 when he dies, the suit complains.

Both policyholders are black. Their policies were originally sold by Supreme Liberty Life Insurance. Reliable took over the policies in 1997, the suit says.

Although Reliable declined to comment on the suit, company officials in the past have explained that it costs more to sell and collect premiums from lots of small insurance policies.

The suit says Reliable deliberately caused some policies to lapse before policyholders died by failing to credit premium payments and hindering clients' efforts to pay premiums.

The suit, filed in U.S. District Court in St. Louis, asks that all black Reliable policyholders be included in the class. The suit demands money damages.

In June, the American General Life and Accident Co. agreed to pay $215 million to settle charges that it charged blacks more than whites for burial insurance.

Reprinted with permission of the *St. Louis Post-Dispatch*. Copyright 2000.

NOTES

Vigilance

PREPARE YOUR MIND

"We shall not fail or falter; we shall not weaken or tire. Neither the sudden shock of battle nor the long-drawn trials of vigilance and exertion will wear us down. Give us the tools and we will finish the job."

Sir Winston Churchill

PREVENTING EXTRACTION

Vigilance

African Americans must become more vigilant—taking complete and total responsibility for protecting their financial interests. The takeover of the lucrative African-American beauty supply industry by Korean Americans is a compelling example of what happens when African Americans fail to recognize and respond to extraction. African-American entrepreneurs stand by frustrated, helplessly watching as Korean business owners take almost complete control of an industry once dominated by African Americans.

While the takeover of the $2.5 billion beauty supply industry is largely attributable to Korean business owners' ability to identify an opportunity and then work in harmony and unison to seize it, tactics used to drive African Americans from the beauty supply industry might violate the Robinson-Patman Act. The Robinson-Patman Act is a federal statute that applies to all persons or businesses involved in commerce or in local activities *affecting* commerce. African-American firms damaged by practices that violate antitrust laws can recoup substantial damages from offending firms.

Section 2. (a) of the Robinson-Patman Act states:

That it shall be unlawful for any person engaged in commerce, in the course of such commerce, either directly or indirectly, to discriminate in price between different purchasers of commodities of like grade and quality, where either or any of

IF YOU'VE GOT MY DOLLAR, I DON'T

PREVENTING EXTRACTION

Vigilance

> the purchases involved in such discrimination are in commerce, where such commodities are sold for use, consumption, or resale within the United States or any Territory thereof or the District of Columbia or any insular possession or other place under the jurisdiction of the United States, and where the effect of such discrimination may be substantially to lessen competition or tend to create a monopoly in any line of commerce, or to injure, destroy, or prevent competition with any person who either grants or knowingly receives the benefit of such discrimination, or with customers of either of them. . . .

The Federal Trade Commission (FTC) and the Antitrust Division of the Department of Justice (DOJ) enforce antitrust laws. While the FTC is empowered to stop companies temporarily from engaging in anticompetitive practices, the Justice Department probes and prosecutes. African Americans should request that FTC and DOJ investigate to determine if practices Korean firms have used to seize control of the African-American beauty supply industry violate antitrust laws.

The following excerpt is from an article, written by Stanley Holmes, that appeared in *The Seattle Times* on September 24, 1995. The article details the manner in which the beauty supply industry has been almost completely extracted from African-American business owners.

PREVENTING EXTRACTION

Vigilance

Cosmetic Changes—Koreans Are Moving into a Beauty Supply Market Once Dominated by African Americans

Richard Park and Brenda Velasquez do business within a block of each other on South Jackson Street, competing for a small piece of a booming $2.5 billion business: selling hair sprays, conditioners, shampoos, rinses, wigs and other beauty-care products to African Americans.

But there the resemblance ends.

Park came to the United States from Seoul, South Korea, in 1975. Soon, he was working for an import-export business. Later, he owned a string of small shops in the Los Angeles and Chicago areas: dry cleaners, a teriyaki restaurant and a beauty-supply store catering to African Americans.

Well-educated and well-connected, Park, 51, bought many of his supplies cheaply from Korean wholesalers and got his financing from Korean banks and friends. He started Western Beauty Supply in the Promenade strip mall on Jackson five years ago.

How's business now?

"Business has been up and down, but over five years business has grown," says Park, who owns another black-beauty-supply shop in Federal Way and has expanded his Seattle store.

Velasquez, who has a college degree and was a former assistant controller for a Sears store in Aurora, started BJ Beauty Supply in the same strip mall in 1981. She later moved it across the street. For years her retail business thrived, but then she watched sales decline as competitors, such as Park, moved in and undercut her prices. She now

IF YOU'VE GOT MY DOLLAR, I DON'T

PREVENTING EXTRACTION

Vigilance

wholesales products to black hair stylists, relying on her ability to market some exclusive products that Korean-owned businesses can't get.

When Velasquez opened her store, she counted more than 10 black-owned beauty-supply businesses across the state that catered to African Americans. Today, she may be the only one left.

How's business?

"We're just hanging in there," she says.

Nationally, Koreans, who have traditionally carved entrepreneurial niches in the small neighborhood grocery and dry-cleaning businesses, now control about 80 percent of the retail end of the black-beauty-supply business, according to Beauty Times, a Korean-language trade journal in St. Louis. Some of the larger shops also sell inexpensive Asian imports, from leather goods to apparel items.

Until recently, African Americans have controlled most of the channels in the black-beauty-supply industry. They still dominate the manufacturing of hair products but are losing control of the wholesale and retail sides of the business just as sales nationwide are growing. . . .

Sales of ethnic hair-care, skin-care and cosmetics products, primarily to African Americans, were up 6 percent in 1992 from 1991, according to a study by Packaged Facts Inc., a New York-based market research firm. Industry sales are expected to grow 6 percent or more annually until 1997.

. . . But it's the Koreans' near monopoly of the black-hair-care business that frustrates African-American merchants, who say they are being squeezed out of one of the few industries they have traditionally dominated.

PREVENTING EXTRACTION

Vigilance

"They know there's a lot of money in it," says Decharlene Williams, owner of Decharlene's Beauty and Boutiques on Madison Street and former president of the Central Area Chamber of Commerce. "They know black people will spend a lot of money on hair, clothes and shoes."

Like many of the issues involving immigration, the story has gone unnoticed without a major conflict. Yet as Asians dominate more small businesses in Seattle's inner city, the question is: Can they thrive and become part of the community without creating the racial tensions that have flared up in the other parts of the country, such as Los Angeles, Chicago and New York City?

The answer is a complicated one, distorted by competition, race and cultural differences. The biggest difference is that Koreans have a tight support network that includes informal access to capital and lots of family and friends to work in the businesses, whereas black merchants can't get support from black consumers.

Koreans, successful at running small inner-city retail stores, entered the black beauty trade because the profits were higher than the razor-thin margins of some of the other businesses.

Korean entrepreneurs applied the same strategy to the black-hair-care business that brought them modest success in other businesses. They work long hours, use family members as a source of cheap labor, establish tight relationships with Korean businesses and wholesalers, and take advantage of their ability to raise financing through Korean banks or family and friends. Many Korean immigrants have a college education and come from a culture that nurtures business as vigorously as the inner city seems to stifle it. . . .

IF YOU'VE GOT MY DOLLAR, I DON'T

PREVENTING EXTRACTION

Vigilance

Cultural factors

Park and Velasquez are no different from any other small-business owner. They want to be successful and make money. But their story illustrates how culture plays a decisive role in the outcome.

Velasquez and other black shopkeepers complain that Korean businesses undercut their competitors by selling below wholesale costs until they have attracted a base of customers, and other owners go out of business.

Park says he studies what his customers need and learns about the products. Price is everything. . . .

Cheaper prices, indeed, do seem to be the reason Korean-owned shops have flourished. But there are other reasons. Korean shop owners benefit from a strong wholesale network that allows them to buy in bulk and cut costs.

Koreans also have what [Steven] Balkin [an economics professor at Roosevelt University in Chicago] calls "social capital," a network of contacts to help new immigrants learn of job opportunities or stores for sale, meet role models and learn how to run a business in the U.S.

"Many of the vendors who will supply you will be Korean also," Balkin says. "They have a vested interest in seeing you succeed. They give you advice and help."

Then there is the kye (pronounced "keh"), which is a common but informal way of raising capital among friends, associates or family. One person leads each kye group, gathering 15 to 25 people who contribute about $500 a month. The total typically reaches $10,000 and often $20,000.

PREVENTING EXTRACTION

Vigilance

Members then can receive the money through a rotation or bidding system and use it to buy or expand their business. The informal ties of kye members can be as binding as a signed loan agreement with a bank. No such thing exists in the black community. Black merchants can't attract that kind of support. They complain that black consumers shop with them last, preferring to go to the Koreans and other business owners first.

"It creates a lot of animosity because the Korean merchants are hostile, but the blacks still shop with them because of the price," says Williams of Decharlene's Beauty and Boutiques. "But when black consumers shop at a black store, they expect more service, they want you to be more polite."

The tight-knit Korean business community also makes it difficult for outsiders to make contacts, sell products or hear about businesses for sale. Most Koreans sell their stores to other Koreans or Asians. . . .

What hurts her [Velasquez] the most, she says, is the lack of a strong support network. She doesn't have the buying power that Koreans have through their distributors and, as Williams points out, support from the community is a problem.

"It hurts us economically," William says. "It's a barrier that we haven't been able to tear down yet."

Korean merchants, for their part, say they, too, are just trying to survive and find economic stability.

"We want to make a successful life here," says Lee of the Beauty Times. "We have more opportunity here. We are the next generation of immigrants. We are no different than the Italians, the Jews and the Irish before us."

Participating in the Rule-making Process

"If you ever live in a country run by a committee, be on the committee."

Author unknown

PREVENTING EXTRACTION

Participating in the Rule-making Process

Another way to prevent extraction is to participate in the rule-making process. While African Americans, like other taxpayers, fund public entities through tax dollars, they often participate minimally in the rule-making process. Participating in the rule-making process can occur in several ways, including (1) *policy formulation*; (2) *Board participation*; (3) *active political involvement*; and (4) *assuming leadership roles in business*.

■ **Policy formulation.** The purpose of any advocacy issue is to resolve a problem. Once the decision is made to alter a process to ensure fairness, you want to be involved in the decision-making process, ensuring that your interests are protected. Your involvement is particularly important since proposals often get modified and changed along the way. Would you allow your competitors to establish rules governing a competition without your input? Of course not! When you are attempting to change the rules, plan to participate in the rule-making process.

■ **Board participation.** Achieving Board participation may require creative thinking, since many of the existing rules have the effect of excluding African Americans. For example, let us assume you must own a building in a downtown historic district to serve on that district's board. Being on the board can be quite advantageous, since many wealth-generating downtown initiatives are discussed by the Board well before they are revealed to the public. While owning a building in the downtown area may seem a reasonable prerequisite to Board participation, it naturally excludes people, since few African Americans have been

PREVENTING EXTRACTION

Participating in the Rule-making Process

privy to contracts and business loans needed to purchase downtown property. **African Americans must operate under the assumption that if there is not sufficient African-American representation, the process is flawed.** We must then take steps necessary to ensure that African-American interests are represented.

■ **Active political involvement.** Politics rule in America. More African Americans should become integrally involved in the political framework by running for political office at all levels and by actively participating behind the scenes in framing political issues and processes. Many seek political office not because of the salary or even their will to serve. Instead, they enter the political arena because political positions are high-profile and wield enormous political power that generally translates into the ability to "do important deals." African Americans should institute a formal process to seek, cultivate, and market candidates who will effectively represent a broad constituency that includes African Americans.

■ **Assuming leadership roles in business.** African Americans can participate in the rule-making process by taking on leadership roles in their workplace and in business organizations, such as the Better Business Bureau, local Chambers of Commerce, and other business organizations. Too often, African Americans operate outside the mainstream, to the detriment of the African-American community.

NOTES

Combatting Opposition

PREPARE YOUR MIND

"I have no friends and no enemies—only competitors."

Aristotle Onassis

COMBATTING OPPOSITION

Empowered African Americans

If you think your competitors are going to sit back and idly watch while you divert to the African-American community the wealth they have enjoyed, you are sorely mistaken. Many of the advances realized in the 1960s and '70s are being steadily chiseled away by competitors who rightly claim that certain programs limit their opportunities, particularly since such opportunities have hitherto almost completely been reserved for competitors. Competitors have not relented in their efforts to take back opportunities diverted to African Americans—and they have made, and continue to make, substantial progress.

Not one bean. One of my favorite passages from the Bible, *2nd Samuel* 23:11, states: "The Philistines had gathered together into a troop, where there was a piece of ground full of lentils. So the people fled from the Philistines. But *he* [one of the villagers] stationed himself in the middle of the field, defended it, and killed the Philistines. So the Lord brought about a great victory."

Imagine a small village of people threatened by the great Philistine army. The entire village fled in fear. One lone villager, however, was unwilling to retreat. He realized that the Philistines would never be content with the bean patch where the lentils grew. He knew that if he gave up the lentil patch, the Philistines would want the livestock, and then the houses, and finally the women and children. The lone villager knew a fight was imminent. The question was, should he fight now or should he fight later? Knowing he would have to fight eventually, he proclaimed that he was not willing to relinquish

COMBATTING OPPOSITION

Empowered African Americans

even one bean. So he stood his ground. He fought and he prevailed.

African Americans can benefit greatly from adopting the "not one bean" stance when it comes to combatting opposition. Competitors' efforts to erode affirmative action have revealed that African Americans must respond immediately to any threat to diminish the gains we make. Once you realize a goal, stand firm to retain it. When your ground is threatened, respond vigorously and immediately. Here are some of the tactics your competitors will employ to oppose your efforts:

- **Stall.** When it comes to African-American concerns, it seems they are never doable—at least not in their entirety, and certainly not now. Decide what is fair and right before you initiate your advocacy efforts. Do not settle for less.

- **You.** You can become competitors' most effective weapon in their fight to prevent change. Many African Americans have in the deepest chambers of their heart accepted the concept of White superiority and African-American inferiority. They believe African Americans do not possess the resources and tools required to change our destiny. As such, each African American must examine his or her own mind: *Do you intrinsically believe a competitor is likely to do a better job than an African American? Do you believe a competitor's product is probably better?* Many African Americans retain psychological scars borne during centuries of racial abuse. Heal yourself. Begin by making positive affirmations about yourself and other African Americans.

COMBATTING OPPOSITION

Empowered African Americans

- **Reports.** Expect reports that are designed to bring dissention and disunity. Investigate all allegations of wrongdoing by African-American organizations or individuals and take the appropriate actions. Never let disappointment, mismanagement, or other similar occurrences interfere with your efforts.

- **Racial coagulation.** It is a defensive strategy competitors employ when African Americans levy charges of racism, inequity, or discrimination. Rather than righting the wrong, energies are instead diverted to covering up or justifying the wrong. The process of *racial coagulation* exerts tremendous social pressure, often enlisting well-intentioned people as co-conspirators in a racial crime. Racial coagulation further punishes victims of racial discrimination.

- **Activity.** Have you ever noticed that African Americans are probably the most studied American ethnic group? Activity creates the illusion that advances are occurring when in fact we are standing still. It is simply an attempt to appease African Americans and conceal lack of progress. African Americans must carefully scrutinize everything and take nothing for granted.

- **Discussion.** *Talk is no substitute for serious action.* It alone will never improve race relations in America. Discussions about diversity and racism make good competitors feel better and African Americans feel empowered. More is required—we must step from the realm of *dialogue* into the realm of *action.*

IF YOU'VE GOT MY DOLLAR, I DON'T

COMBATTING OPPOSITION

Empowered African Americans

- **Process revisions.** Once you have devised and presented a plan to correct a problem, you can be assured your competitor will attempt to diminish the effectiveness of your proposal by suggesting alterations. Closely scrutinize every change your competitor suggests to make sure changes do not compromise the goals you seek to obtain.

- **Erosion.** Many advances intended for minorities have instead been eroded by remedies designed to aid White females. African Americans and women have two very different experiences. While White women have also been subject to disparate treatment, quite a few have amassed wealth through their husbands and fathers. As such, the remedies and goals for African Americans should be significantly more aggressive than remedies designed for White women.

- **Counterfeits that appear to offer opportunity but instead limit opportunity.** Special learning programs are often presented to African-American parents as a way of helping their children who are experiencing learning difficulties. Today, disproportionate numbers of African-American youths are in remedial learning programs. Many students enrolled in these programs are literally discarded by the education system. As a result, they lose faith in themselves, believing they are incapable of excelling academically. **Closely scrutinize programs that are reportedly designed to help.**

COMBATTING OPPOSITION

Empowered African Americans

- **Introduce complexities.** Competitors introduce complexities to mask erosion. Affirmative action programs in the contracting arena are an excellent example. First, the courts required disparity studies. Next, they questioned the data used in the studies—including census data, which are used in almost every major study in America. The courts then proceeded to require regression analysis in an attempt to quantify how much of the disparity African Americans experience is attributable to discrimination. The saga continues, with the goal being to completely remove all effectiveness from race-based remedies such as affirmative action programs. African Americans must unravel the complexities, decipher the plan so it is apparent to all, and then engage in vigorous efforts to retain economic, social, and political gains.

- **Exhaust your resources.** Competitors can use the extensive resources they have at their disposal to exhaust African Americans' attempts to bring about change. They can literally tie you up for years by hiring expensive lawyers. Since it is sometimes difficult to match competitors' resources, learn to turn your weaknesses into strengths.

- **Create major upsets to diminish and discourage.** After reading this book, many African Americans will propel from the start line with determination and vigor. This race, however, is not necessarily for the swift sprinter; it is a long-distance race for the true winner who has the soul, heart, and mind

COMBATTING OPPOSITION

Empowered African Americans

to succeed. Just when you believe you have won on major initiatives, your competitor will create earth-shattering setbacks. You can stay down—or get up and start the race again, with even greater determination and vigor.

- **Ignore you and minimize your issues.** At the outset, do not expect competitors to take you seriously. When you begin challenging competitors' actions, they might at first dismiss you, ignore you, and otherwise discount your concerns. Persist nevertheless! Competitors will soon discover that you are committed and determined to benefit from the vast wealth America's economic system offers.

- **Allege preference.** Many African-American managers and policy-makers are hostile competitors. They deny African Americans opportunities in their attempt to demonstrate to others they are not showing preference to their "own kind." These decision-makers are also hostile competitors and should be treated accordingly.

- **Unresponsive political candidates.** African Americans often express fervent support for candidates simply because they are African Americans. These same politicians often completely ignore the needs of the African-American community. Yet the community reelects them time and time again, simply because they are African-American. African Americans must began electing candidates based upon their *demonstrated willingness* to get involved and forward initiatives that concern African Americans. When

COMBATTING OPPOSITION

Empowered African Americans

politicians—whether competitors or African Americans—
ignore our needs, we must exact a political price by
opposing such candidates and actively endorsing candidates
who respond to African-American interests. If none of the
candidates represent your interests, introduce a candidate
who does. Your competitors select and promote candidates
all the time.

■ **Retain empathy.** Many African Americans who are successful
grow impatient with those who have "not arrived." These
African Americans are sometimes more harsh on other
African Americans than on hostile competitors. Remember,
prosperous African Americans, that while your blessings
might in large part be attributable to your determination,
hard work, and smart choices, your destiny is in other ways
like the draw of a card. Had the right people not entered
your path or had your life been otherwise different, the
blessings you now enjoy might belong to another.

Soaring Ahead

PREPARE YOUR MIND

"Do not follow where the path may lead. Go instead where there is no path and leave a trail."

Author unknown

SOARING AHEAD

Empowered African Americans

- **Value differences.** There are many types of African-American leaders who employ different tactics in their pursuit of equal opportunity and fair play for African Americans. Some are *diplomats*; some are *grassroots advocates* who encourage boycotts, blockades, sit-ins, and other acts of civil disobedience; and some are *highly controversial*. Most, however, contribute to African Americans' quest for equal opportunity. So value their differences.

- **Abandon political correctness.** Because of advances brought about by the civil rights movement in the 1950s and '60s, we have significant numbers of African Americans who are more educated, affluent, and sophisticated. Often, African Americans prefer to appear politically correct, which is **doing what is palatable for the setting rather than communicating candidly about tough issues**. Just imagine: If Rosa Parks had decided to be politically correct on December 1, 1955, in Montgomery, Alabama, African Americans might still be sitting at the back of the bus.

  Our competitors are not in our position, so they can afford to be politically correct. You, however, are attempting to catch up. When you encounter racial discrimination that limits you economically, call it what it is: racial discrimination. Then do something about it.

IF YOU'VE GOT MY DOLLAR, I DON'T

SOARING AHEAD

Empowered African Americans

- **Jealousy and envy.** Limited opportunity can create division. Remember, all African Americans will not rise at the same rate. Accept it and find joy in others' successes. One day, the success you celebrate will be yours.

- **Stop trying to make competitors understand.** Too often, African Americans expend tremendous effort trying to make competitors see their viewpoint. Many competitors are incapable of identifying or empathizing with racism because they are simply too far removed from the experience.

  Accept that some competitors will never value or appreciate your viewpoint. Your goal is advancing economically—not enlisting the empathy of competitors.

- **Devote resources to improving African Americans' economic status.** Spend time on promoting your interests. No organization or leader can move African Americans forward alone. It takes many people who are willing to devote their time and resources to changing the financial and social status of African Americans. Contributing finances to organizations that support African-American advocacy efforts is "self-enlightened interest."

SOARING AHEAD

Empowered African Americans

- **Be aware of how others mischaracterize to allay concerns.**
  Suppose a news report alleges that more is spent per
  student in inner-city schools than is spent per child in
  suburban schools. Most African Americans would accept
  this statement as fact. Do not. Ask to see the formula
  revealing how this fact was determined. If the school
  district has outdated facilities and equipment, the inner-
  city school may have extremely high maintenance costs
  compared to schools that are new, state-of-the-art facilities.
  While more may be spent per child, the expenditure may
  not be contributing to a quality education. Always ask the
  second- and third-level questions. As Malcolm X would say,
  don't be "hoodwinked and bamboozled."

- **Recognize substitutions.** Substitutions are intended to divert
  African Americans' focus from the real issues. Many
  corporations contribute large gifts to African-American
  institutions and sponsor major events in the African-American
  community to posture themselves as community allies. While
  these gifts are beneficial and much appreciated, they are no
  substitute for real opportunity. With high-paying jobs and
  lucrative contracts, African Americans can support themselves
  and their own communities.

- **Reveal the power of your vote.** Vote in every election!
  Candidates will soon discover that you are a power to be
  reckoned with. Only then will they begin to work for your
  vote.

IF YOU'VE GOT MY DOLLAR, I DON'T

SOARING AHEAD

Empowered African Americans

- **Participate in every census.** Take great care to complete census forms accurately. Additionally, African Americans should become partners in every phase of the census process.

- **Closely examine every measure that garners political opposition.** According to the U.S. Constitution, the federal government every 10 years must complete a full census, known as the decennial census. One reason for conducting the census is to provide the House of Representatives with the information it needs to apportion its 435 seats among the states. When performing congressional apportionment, Congress reserves 50 seats, assigning one to each state. It then assigns remaining seats to the various states, based upon census counts. Armed with census data, state legislators can commence redistricting, redrawing both congressional and state congressional boundaries. To ensure a more accurate census in year 2000, the U.S. Census Bureau planned to use statistical sampling to augment census counts, particularly of traditionally undercounted populations such as African Americans, Hispanic Americans, and Native Americans. Yet many politicians vehemently opposed the Census Bureau's plan, challenging it in court. On January 25, 1999, the Supreme Court sided with congressional leaders, ruling that statistically altered census counts could not be used for *congressional apportionment*.

SOARING AHEAD

Empowered African Americans

Why, you may ask, would congressional leaders oppose a statistically augmented count? Because significant changes in congressional boundaries can dramatically alter the demographic makeup of a representative's constituency, thus jeopardizing the representative's reelection. While congressional representatives concern themselves with political costs, African Americans and other minorities continue to forfeit funds their communities desperately need. Since an accurate census means more federal funds for African-American communities, African Americans and other citizens should work to secure legislation that requires the use of statistically augmented census data as the basis for allocating government funds.

- **Be ethical in your dealings.** Many African-Americans have mistakenly believed they can engage in the same infractions competitors engaged in for years without scrutiny. African Americans must accept that they are held to a different standard. As such, they must do what is right, what is appropriate, and what is fair. Besides, there is inherent value in doing what is honest and right.

- **Don't play the race card.** When you have not towed the rope, do not allege racial discrimination. Persons who wrongly allege racism do everyone, especially African Americans, a disservice. If, however, you are the subject of racial discrimination, proclaim it loudly and often.

- **Promote a climate of freedom and prosperity.** This struggle will not be easy. It is, however, the only alternative if African

IF YOU'VE GOT MY DOLLAR, I DON'T

SOARING AHEAD

Empowered African Americans

Americans are ever to live a life of true freedom and financial opportunity. Offer encouragement and willingly take an active role, even if the matter does not affect you directly. The day may arrive when it is you who needs support.

- **Don't let your wealth be superior to you.** The greatest assurance of positive quality of life is a good attitude—not money. Learn to be happy no matter what your station in life. Make the most of each day. Remember: This is a competition, not a war!

- **Seize the moment.** Timing can be everything. Too often, African Americans forego excellent opportunities because we belabor our decision-making. Study the opportunity and associated risks. Get excellent advice. Make your decision and act.

- **Display your indignation.** America remembers in great detail the violence and mayhem that followed the acquittal of police officers in the Rodney King incident. It seems, however, that every high-profile incident of police brutality is soon followed by a police chief, investigator, and sometimes even the victim's family encouraging calm in the face of justified anger. Is a display of righteous indignation appropriate? If so, when is such a display appropriate?

Perhaps this question is best answered by reviewing an excerpt from an Associated Press (AP) release on July 13, 2000:

SOARING AHEAD

Empowered African Americans

Feds launch investigation of police beating

PHILADELPHIA (AP)—The U.S. Justice Department launched an investigation Thursday of the videotaped beating of a black suspect by police officers following a stolen car chase and shootout.

A dozen officers—black and white—were involved in Wednesday's beating of Thomas Jones, 30.

The confrontation was captured by videotape from a news helicopter and broadcast around the nation, reminiscent of the 1991 Rodney King case that ignited rioting in Los Angeles after four white officers were acquitted of state charges. Two of the LAPD officers were eventually convicted of federal civil rights charges.

"For people to start making comparisons to Rodney King, I just think is outrageous," Police Commissioner John Timoney told ABC's "Good Morning America." "He is resisting throughout. Now, does that justify the force? We won't know until we interview the officers."

The city's black mayor cautioned against jumping to conclusions.

"As inflammatory as this tape might be, we have to keep in mind that the police were in the process of apprehending a criminal suspect who had resisted a number of attempts to arrest him and who had shot a police officer," Mayor John F. Street said. "The tape raises some questions, but the tape also doesn't show everything that was going on.". . .

Bertha Jones, 40, was sitting on her porch when she saw the first confrontation. She said she saw the suspect jump over a gate with his hands in the air, as if to surrender." . . .

Reprinted with permission of The Associated Press.

SOARING AHEAD

Empowered African Americans

While such incidents warrant an investigation to determine how the incident escalated from the initial chase to a police shootout and subsequent car chase, the videotaped beating requires no further investigation. Simply stated, it was excessive force. Had Thomas Jones instead been a dangerous animal that America witnessed being kicked multiple times while it lay on the ground with four bullet wounds, the party committing the vicious act would have been arrested by police on the spot and charged with animal abuse. (As it happens, subsequent ballistics tests indicated that Thomas Jones did not shoot the police officer—who actually was shot by another officer!)

Don't abandon your anger, and don't always exhibit patience. Some actions demand an immediate and angry response. When used properly, *sustained anger* can be a powerful advocacy tool that makes politicians and community leaders take notice. **Anger, however, is not synonymous with violence.**

NOTES

What You Can Do

PREPARE YOUR MIND

"You're either part of the solution or part of the problem."

Eldridge Cleaver

WHAT YOU CAN DO

Get Involved

They said nothing. Someone knew the act in progress violated the most fundamental laws of humanity. Yet they said nothing and they did nothing. They watched as the noose was placed around the Black man's neck, his body lifted high, and his legs kicking violently until life drained from his body. Standing there, riddled with conviction and guilt, they continued to do nothing and say nothing.

The nature of who you are. If you are like most people reading this book, you probably consider yourself an equitable competitor. But are you—really? Today, like so many people long ago, those who deem themselves ethical observe vicious acts, racist acts among them—in their workplaces, their communities, and their schools. Yet they do nothing and they say nothing.

Being ethical involves a deliberate commitment to make life better in America for *all*. It means getting involved and standing for what is right—even when you must stand alone.

IF YOU'VE GOT MY DOLLAR, I DON'T

WHAT YOU CAN DO

Religious Institutions and Leaders

- **Live according to your faith.** Americans need to assess their racial attitudes in a spiritual context.

  Clergy. Racial abuse is a moral and religious issue. By speaking *frequently, candidly,* and *openly* about the sin of racism, religious leaders such as priests, ministers, and rabbis can bridge the racial divide and help repair the hurt and damage that discrimination causes.

  Congregations. According to published poll results, more than 80 percent of the American population professes to hold Christian values. Too often, however, those values do not encompass racial dealings. *Proverbs* 16:11 states that God demands fairness in every business dealing. Whether you are Christian or Jewish, a follower of Islam or a traveler along another spiritual path, this mandate applies to you— and it means you should deal fairly with all, including African Americans.

WHAT YOU CAN DO

Religious Institutions and Leaders

- **Encourage the U.S. Government to pay reparations to African Americans.** Recompense and restitution are godly mandates. America owes a debt to African Americans—and it is time America pays. *Leviticus* 6:4–5 states:

  > . . . he shall restore what he has stolen, or the thing which he has extorted, or what was delivered to him for safekeeping, or the lost thing which he found, or all that about which has sworn falsely. He shall restore its full value, add one-fifth more to it, and give it to whomever it belongs, on the day of his trespass offering.

  Restitution is not an option. It is the prelude to improved race relations in America. Monetary restoration is a tangible expression of America's repentance for the crimes it has committed against people of African descent. True, heartfelt forgiveness will not occur until there is reparation. African Americans must be made whole!

IF YOU'VE GOT MY DOLLAR, I DON'T

WHAT YOU CAN DO

Equitable Competitors

Ethical competitors can improve national race relations by taking a proactive stance, insisting on equality and fairness in every circumstance in which they are involved. Here are some specific suggestions:

- **Evaluate occurrences solely on the facts.** Many competitors are simply incapable of identifying or empathizing with the destructive nature of racism, since it has not hindered their progress. Commit to evaluating every occurrence objectively. Consider how you would view the matter if you were African-American and in the same situation. When actions are unfair, say they are unfair.

- **Adopt zero tolerance for disparate treatment.** Allegations of discrimination are often so frequent that competitors simply write them off. Decide, nevertheless, that as a member of this great society, you will adopt the same intolerance of racial abuse as America has adopted with regard to child or spousal abuse.

- **Refuse to engage in racial coagulation.** While African Americans have a radar for disparate treatment, most competitors cannot identify discrimination unless it is flagrant and blatant. Determine that you will not take sides until the facts are in, even when it involves a friend or person you admire. It takes real character to insist on what is right, no matter who is involved.

WHAT YOU CAN DO

Equitable Competitors

- **Avoid becoming defensive.** Allegations of racism create great divides. They separate and polarize. Recognize that allegations of racism against a person in your race is not a personal indictment against you. By insisting on fairness and equity, you can become a part of the healing process.

- **Own the problem.** You may detest the notion of accepting responsibility for the transgressions of your ancestors. If you, however, benefitted from your ancestors' gross transgressions, then you bear some responsibility for their actions, especially when those actions involved crimes against people.

- **Understand how unfair competition works.** Discrimination is seldom blatant. It more commonly occurs as insidious comments designed to instill doubt about capability; snide comments about performance that have no basis in fact; mischaracterizations to disguise wrongful intent; and subtle actions that deliver some element of privilege or advantage.

- **Get involved!** When you refuse to get involved, you become an enabler of racial discrimination. So get involved. Take an active role in advocacy efforts and, like African Americans, react with indignation when rules are applied in an unfair manner. Become a pillar of democracy by cultivating a community where decency, ethics, and fair play are the only acceptable rules of the game.

Freedom Begins with You

When the avenues of wealth are opened to us we will become educated and wealthy, and then the roughest-looking colored man that you ever saw . . . will be pleasanter than the harmonies of Orpheus, and black will be a very pretty color. It will make our jargon, wit—our words, oracles; flattery will then take the place of slander, and you will find no prejudice in the Yankee whatsoever.

These are the words of John Swett Rock, who in 1864 became the first African-American attorney admitted to the bar of the U.S. Supreme Court.

FREEDOM BEGINS WITH YOU

Empowered African Americans

The following is an excerpt from *Chronology on the History of Slavery*, 1619–1789, compiled by Eddie Becker (1999):

> In America, with only a few early and insignificant exceptions, all slaves were Africans, and almost all Africans were slaves. This placed the label of inferiority on black skin and on African culture. In other societies, it had been possible for a slave who obtained his freedom to take his place in his society with relative ease. In America, however, when a slave became free, he was still obviously an African. The taint of inferiority clung to him. Not only did white America become convinced of white superiority and black inferiority, but it strove to impose these racial beliefs on the Africans themselves. Slave masters gave a great deal of attention to the *education and training of the ideal slave*. In general there were five steps in molding the character of such a slave: ***strict discipline, a sense of his own inferiority, belief in the master's superior power, acceptance of the master's standards, and, finally, a deep sense of his own helplessness and dependence.***
> [Author's bold and italic type.]

IF YOU'VE GOT MY DOLLAR, I DON'T

FREEDOM BEGINS WITH YOU

Empowered African Americans

African Americans: Are you among those who believe the problems African Americans endure are too significant to change? Are you among those who say African Americans will never work together? Do you believe that the goals in this book cannot be attained?

*If so, ask yourself if you embrace the **helplessness** and **dependency** that slave owners so long ago tried to ensure would live on in you.*

The future is yours to define!

NOTES

Taking Care of Business

I want to arise and partake of all that God has awaiting me. But receiving requires of me great discipline, determination, and a willingness to learn. I shall fortify my dreams with a plan, and I shall become a doer—moving forward and realizing my vision with each step. For without a plan, I am simply a dreamer—always wanting and never having.

CREATING A FINANCIAL PLAN

Empowered African Americans

The most successful people in life are people who plan. Plan to go to college, and you will go to college. Plan to buy a house, and you will own a house. Plan to have savings, and you will have savings. Plan nothing, and you will have nothing.

To prosper financially, you must create a financial plan and follow it. The first step in financial planning is establishing a budget. Many people embark upon the path of budgeting with vigor, only to succumb to defeat. Budgeting can be a real challenge, particularly if you are accustomed to spending at will.

Budget even if you do not have enough money to take care of your expenses. Remember, however, that learning to manage money is a process—a skill developed over time. So do not give up, no matter how many times you seem to fail. Keep trying until you manage poverty, stress, and financial burdens right out of your life!

CREATING A FINANCIAL PLAN

Empowered African Americans

There are many ways you can learn about the budgeting process. You can visit your local library, search out materials on the Internet, or enroll in a money management class at your local college. The following are some sources I have come to appreciate when it comes to money management:

- **The Internet.** You can find many tools on the Internet under the topic of personal budgeting. Also, visit our website at **www.gotmydollar.com** to review a range of information to help you prosper financially.

- **Bookstores.** During my visits to a local bookstore I found a number of books that provide much information about the budgeting process. Most of these books also include the forms and tools needed for budgeting.

- **Computer software.** There are many low-cost software products that you can use for the budgeting process, such as Microsoft Money and Quicken. Visit software stores and consult computer magazines that provide software product reviews and evaluations.

- **Local churches.** There are excellent money management programs, available at many neighborhood churches, that teach managing finances from a biblical perspective.

NOTES

IF YOU'VE GOT MY DOLLAR, I DON'T

READING LIST

- *Black Wealth/White Wealth: A New Perspective on Racial Inequality*, by Melvin L. Oliver and Thomas M. Shapiro. This Routledge publication examines how systemic barriers prevent African Americans from accumulating the significant private wealth Whites amass.

- *Language in Thought and Action*, by S. I. Hayakawa. This Harcourt Brace Jovanovich publication is an all-time favorite of mine. Years after first reading this book, I find it still helps shape my opinions. *Language in Thought and Action* reminds me every day that "allness" seldom applies: All White people are not racist; all Asians are not academic achievers; all Germans were not Nazis; and so on.

- *The Rage of a Privileged Class*, by Ellis Cose. From HarperPerennial comes this book that offers insightful vignettes on the challenges "successful" African Americans continue to face because of the color of their skin.

- *Thurgood Marshall: American Revolutionary*, by Juan Williams. Published by Times Books, this epic biography of one of the towering figures in the civil rights movement is highly detailed and compellingly readable. The author takes special note of Marshall's landmark legal victory in *Brown v. Board of Education*, which paved the way for desegregated schools and the reclaiming of basic human rights for African Americans.

ORDER FORM

Please send _____ copies of *The Physics of Money: If You've Got My Dollar, I Don't.* Each copy is $25.00 (US dollars) plus shipping and handling:

USA: $4.00 for the first book; $2.00 for each additional copy to the same address.

International (US dollars): $9.00 for the first book; $5.00 for each additional copy to the same address.

I WISH TO PAY BY:

❑ Check or money order payable to *Lordes Publishing, Inc.* Add shipping and handling charge(s). For books shipped to Missouri, please also add $1.80 in state sales tax for each book ordered.

❑ Visa or ❑ MasterCard. Shipping and handling charge(s) will be added. For each book shipped to Missouri, $1.80 in state sales tax will also be added.

_____

Signature of Cardholder

| | | | | | | | | | | | | | | | | | | | | | | | | | |

Card Number   Expiration Date

PLEASE SEND THE BOOK(S) TO:

Name _____

Address _____ Apt/Ste _____

City _____ State _____ ZIP _____

Telephone _____ E-mail _____

Here are ways you can order:

🖹 Fax the completed form to **1–314–725–9755**. Include your credit card information.

☎ Phone your order to **1–314–725–9753**. Have your order and credit card information ready.

✉ Place an online order at **www.gotmydollar.com** and include your credit card information.

🖻 Mail the completed form to **The Physics of Money, PO Box 50331, Clayton, MO 63105–5331**. Enclose your check or money order, if applicable.